Gender and Agricultural Development

T0163521

GENDER and AGRICULTURAL DEVELOPMENT

Surveying the Field

EDITED BY

Helen Kreider Henderson with Ellen Hansen

THE UNIVERSITY OF ARIZONA PRESS / TUCSON

First printing 1995
The University of Arizona Press
Copyright © 1995
The Arizona Board of Regents
All rights reserved

∞ This book is printed on acid-free, archival-quality paper.
Manufactured in the United States of America

Library of Congress Cataloging-in-Publication Data

Gender and agricultural development : surveying the field / edited by
    Helen Kreider Henderson with Ellen Hansen.
        p.   cm.
    Includes index.
    ISBN 0-8165-1542-5 (alk. paper)
    ISBN 0-8165-1565-4 (pbk.: alk. paper)
    1. Women in agriculture—Developing countries.   2. Women farmers—
Developing countries.   3. Women in development—Developing
countries.   I. Henderson, Helen Kreider.   II. Hansen, Ellen.
    HD6073.A272D44   1995   94-18774
    331.4'83'091724—dc20   CIP
British Cataloguing-in-Publication Data
A catalogue record for this book is available from the British Library.

CONTENTS

CONTRIBUTORS

Catherine Besteman is an Assistant Professor of Anthropology at Colby College. She received her Ph.D. in anthropology from the University of Arizona. Based on her fieldwork in Portugal and Somalia, she has published articles on land tenure, agriculture, and gender in *Economic Development and Cultural Change* and in *Africa*. She is currently working on a book about stratification, social identity, and political disintegration in Somalia.

Ellen Hansen is Graduate Research Associate in the Women in Development Program of the Bureau of Applied Research in Anthropology and a Ph.D. candidate in the Department of Geography and Regional Development at the University of Arizona. She served as a Peace Corps volunteer in Ecuador, working with indigenous farmers of the Andes and focusing on women's groups. She has conducted research in Mexico and Arizona on migration and women's status in the household.

Helen Kreider Henderson is the head of the Women in Development Program and is an Assistant Research Anthropologist in the Bureau of Applied Research in Anthropology at the University of Arizona. She received her Ph.D. in anthropology from the University of California, Berkeley. She has conducted research on gender issues in agriculture in Niger, Burkina Faso, Mauritania, Chad, and Egypt, and on women and religion in Nigeria. Her publications include essays and reports on women farmers in the Sahel and women's roles in livestock production. Her essays on women in agricultural education, female-headed households, and applied research with female farmers have appeared in *International Education, Urban Anthropology,* and the *NAPA Bulletin*.

Elizabeth Howard-Powell holds the position of Program Coordinator for the State of Texas Governor's Executive Development Program. In this capacity she coordinates leadership training programs for senior executives in Texas state agencies and universities. Howard-Powell holds an M.A. degree in Applied Anthropology from the University of Arizona and is currently a M.Ed. candidate in the Human Resources Development Program at the University of Texas at Austin.

Judith Ann Warner is Associate Professor of Sociology at Texas A & M International University. She received her Ph.D. in Sociology from the University of Arizona. Her recent publications include essays and reports on the sociological impact of *maquiladoras,* family stress among Mexican women domestics, the socio-demographic characteristics of the South Texas border, and entries in the *African American Encyclopedia.* She is currently researching Hillary Clinton's treatment by the press.

ACKNOWLEDGMENTS

The insights of women farmers in the Third World form the substance of the research presented here. These farmers, and the researchers whose observations and analyses of their work are reviewed in this volume, together are changing the ways we think about development. In the early days of research on gender issues in agriculture, the researchers' determination to convert materials from project field reports into scholarly publications enabled advocates for more equitable development to argue their case from well-founded positions. Many of these researchers are cited in this book, although the body of knowledge is building so rapidly that it is impossible to acknowledge everyone who has contributed to it.

I would particularly like to thank those people who wanted to see research findings on women in development issues made available to a wider audience and who encouraged me to undertake a review of such work. Among them are Kay Davies and John Hourihan, formerly of the Women in Development Office of the Agency for International Development in Washington, D.C., and Carlos Vélez Ibáñez and Kathleen Mac. Thompson of the Bureau of Applied Research in Anthropology at the University of Arizona. Judy Voss, also of the bureau, has shown unfailing patience and good humor in preparing various versions of the manuscript. Many thanks must be given to the contributors—Ellen Hansen, Judith Warner, Catherine Besteman and Elizabeth Howard-Powell—for their careful and insightful research.

A concept paper funded by a grant from the Office of Women in Development of the U.S. Agency for International Development to the Bureau of Applied Research in Anthropology (AID Grant No. DPE-0100-

C-00-5008-00) was used as background material for the *Gender Issues in Agriculture and Natural Resource Management* volume in the Gender Manual Series (Russo et al. 1989) and was an impetus for the creation of this book. The Women in Development Office is not responsible for and has not reviewed this manuscript, nor have present or former members of that office.

INTRODUCTION

This book covers major issues in the field of women in development as they apply to agricultural planning from the local to the international level. The authors' reviews of materials on women's agricultural work include differing analytical perspectives from the early 1970s to the early 1990s. Our goal is to present the major arguments and their justification for considering women as prime actors in agriculture in the Third World.

Our focus is practical and applied; we intend to provide information on locating and incorporating materials on gender-related agricultural issues into development planning, research, and training. Development practitioners may use the book as part of training programs to provide substantive, multilocational evidence for women's significant contributions to agriculture and to ensure the appropriate collection of gender disaggregated data during field research. In addition to development planners, the book is addressed to students and faculty in applied social sciences such as anthropology, geography, and economics, and to those wishing to integrate gender-relevant materials into their courses on agricultural systems, natural resource management, and home economics.

Research on women in agriculture has affected how women are perceived as active agents of change by providing new approaches to data collection, definitions of work, analyses of relations between home work and farm work, the relationships between household and individual budgets, gender-differentiated resource control and allocation, and girls' and women's opportunities for training (see Tinker 1990). This expanding body of research needs to be more widely disseminated to audiences in the development community and to students and faculty in fields related to agriculture. The issues noted above, and others, are summarized in this volume in order to make them more easily accessible.

The political and theoretical frameworks implied in the book are ones that can be adopted by members of the policy-making establishment; they have, indeed, been accepted by most international development agencies with varying degrees of commitment. In addition, by identifying women's lack of political and economic resources and their struggle to overcome these limitations, these frameworks can serve the strategic interests of women in changing political and social contexts (for a discussion of practical versus strategic interests, see Alvarez 1990; Molyneaux 1985; and Moser 1989).

Gender and *development* are two terms used frequently in this book, but their meanings require some clarification here. The term *gender* refers to the social, cultural, and historical construction of male and female roles, which though "related to biological roles are not coterminous with them" (Monk and Momsen 1994:14). In the 1970s and early 1980s the term *Women in Development* was used to make visible the work, needs, and contributions of women in Third World countries, much of which was invisible in the writing of socioeconomic analysts or was subsumed under discussions of the household. The contemporary use of the term *gender,* however, has the advantage of stressing the variability of women's experiences—including variability by class, race, and belief systems—and the relationships between women's and men's experiences (see Moser 1989 and Rathgeber 1990).

Development has been defined as the process of improving the quality of people's lives by raising their standard of living, increasing their choice in consumer goods and services, and enhancing their self-esteem through institutions that promote human dignity (Todaro 1985:580). In contrast to this market-oriented approach, critics of Western development models call for "a dialogue among cultures" concerning social and environmental values and the equitable distribution of wealth (Goulet 1992:472). The United Nations Development Program (UNDP) suggests that human development is a process of enlarging people's choices, especially choices that enable people to have health, longevity, education, and a decent standard of living. Additional important choices include political freedom and human rights (Young 1993). In any definition of development, gender must be a critical element in evaluating global value systems, and women's voices and experiences must be made an integral part of the call for human rights.

The term *development planner* refers to individuals who investigate, anywhere from the community to the international level, the opportunities, needs, and feasibility of economic, social, and political intervention aimed at raising the standard of living in a community or state. Little development planning has taken into account the large and increasing body of knowledge regarding gender issues in development. This book is one attempt to provide an accessible review and synthesis of the major issues for those who specialize in this work.

Throughout this book, the term *Third World countries* refers to those less-industrialized, lower-income countries that were seen (when the term *Third World* was coined) as being in contrast to First World (capitalist) and Second World (socialist) countries. Many Third World nations eschewed allegiance to First or Second World power blocs. Using one term to refer to the widely varying countries and regions of the world that fit into the category as it is used in this book is obviously inadequate. By referring to the Third World instead of the less-developed countries or developing countries, however, we acknowledge the various levels of development within the nations of the world and the resulting divisions between advantaged and disadvantaged groups, which are not confined to higher- or lower-income countries but are found throughout the world.

The literature reviewed in these chapters both calls attention to women's work in order to improve women's access to technology and training, as in the modernization model (Rathgeber 1990:491), and challenges existing development paradigms. In making arguments for the greater efficiency of production efforts that include women, existing inequities are exposed. When, for example, the authors review suggestions for enhancing farm women's productivity in fields with low productivity, they are also pointing out inequities in land distribution and economic benefits relative to women farmers. Thus we view women not only as attempting to "integrate into existing systems," as in the classic Women in Development approach, but also as envisioning significant changes in political and economic structures.

The issues discussed in these chapters present women's experiences and local knowledge and allude to gender and class inequities that farming women face (Rathgeber 1990:500). The discussions provide a framework within which community development planners and policy makers can structure the debate on these issues and possibly have an impact on national development strategies. Although the authors do not specifically address class or ethnic status as factors in international development, a focus on people on the lower end of the socioeconomic scale, who are often the objects and increasingly the initiators of agricultural change, is implicit in the chapters.

No longer do Women in Development scholars and planners hold an excessively optimistic view of the role of information in changing inequities in the world. Instead, there is a greater awareness of the resistance of diverse social and economic institutions—from the family to the global conglomerates—to the empowerment of an existing compliant, undervalued labor force. Sobering also are the effects of macroeconomic world trends associated with labor migration, increasing population pressure on limited arable land, and structural adjustment policies, with their emphasis on producing export crops and reducing subsidized government services, especially education (Gladwin 1993).

Still, information about the lives, experiences, and knowledge of women in Third World countries is continually being gathered and reported. In this volume we have assembled a review and bibliography of important and valuable works covering a wide range of research on women and agricultural development over the past twenty-five years. The information compiled here provides development practitioners, students, women's centers, and others interested in the issues with a guide to the literature and resources available and a focused discussion of rural women in Third World countries. The bibliography, which includes sources that provide a historical overview of the evolution of thought on issues concerning women and development from the 1970s to the present, is extensive but not exhaustive. While we recognize that information alone will not change women's lives, it is our hope that assembling it in this form will help illuminate the needs of women and identify action alternatives.

ORGANIZATION OF THE BOOK

The organizational approach followed here analyzes issues under the following categories: the gender division of labor, time allocation, access to land, income generation, credit, appropriate technology, agricultural extension, and out-migration. These categories have been developed by others in the field (see, for example, Boserup 1970; Dixon 1980; Overholt et al. 1985; Pala 1976). The analytical categories direct our attention to agricultural tasks in terms of (a) responsibilities associated with gender; (b) time allocation per task in relation to other associated tasks; (c) gender differences in access to and control of basic resources such as land, income, credit, appropriate technology, and training; and (d) the impact of heavy out-migration on women farmers. These categories, each of which interacts with the others, shape the actions and opportunities of both women and men.

Using the categories, we have reviewed the conceptual and research literature on women in agriculture in the Third World with an emphasis on design and implementation. Each chapter contains a detailed discussion of the implications of gender research for policies and projects. Numerous examples clearly indicate why and how viewing women as active participants in agricultural change can lead to more successful outcomes.

The book is divided into two major parts: Part I, on agricultural systems, and Part II, on applications of the gender-focused approach to special project areas. In Part I the contributors explore women's access to productive resources. We argue that acknowledging women's contributions to agricultural production is the first step toward changing inequitable labor and distribution patterns. Because excellent gender-relevant data are available on agricultural systems, the major organizational categories outlined above (gender division of labor, time allocation, income generation, etc.) are explored in depth, each in a separate chapter.

Part II consists of chapters on three specific applications of gender-focused research relevant to development projects: livestock management, water management, and agroforestry—all of which have received considerable international development attention. Each chapter employs the conceptual framework developed in Part I and is organized under categories that are explored there—for example, the gender division of labor, time allocation, access to land, appropriate technology, and extension and training. An additional category, community planning, explores some women's initiatives in each topical area.

It is our intention that people who are working on a specific aspect of a development activity will be able to go directly to the chapter most relevant to their interests. For example, those dealing with land reform may want to turn to the chapter on access to land, while those working with an irrigation project may select the chapter on water management.

Although the various agricultural topics are easily accessible, and certain aspects of each topic are quite distinct, we wish to emphasize that the basic topics are interrelated and that in a wider sense no one topic in agricultural development can be viewed in isolation. The gender division of labor, time allocation, and access to resources are themes that appear throughout all the chapters, and they each affect and are affected by migration issues. Therefore, although each topic can be approached independently, effective development recognizes the need for integrated, long-range planning that takes all these topics into consideration.

Finally, we want to emphasize our hope that the topical reviews will aid planners and local communities in identifying and prioritizing their needs and goals. Involving women in community planning means building on knowledge of the existing gender division of labor and the existing social class systems. It means contacting women at places and times convenient to their busy schedules, working with local and regional women's organizations, directing incentives and training toward women, and ensuring that development initiatives do not undercut women's already severely stressed resources.

Helen Kreider Henderson

Part I

Agricultural Systems

1

THE GENDER DIVISION OF LABOR

Helen Kreider Henderson

As used in this book, the term "gender division of labor" refers to the so-cially ascribed assignment of work and allocation of resources on the basis of a categorical designation of individuals as female or male. The gender division of labor is a dynamic concept because gender roles are shaped by changing socioeconomic and historical-cultural factors, including class, ethnicity, and race. The gender division of labor has, however, at times been used similarly to the more biologically based "sexual division of labor" to relegate women's participation in the economy to more passive, less pro-ductive, and therefore less valuable activities than men's (Moser 1989:1813). Women's work is to some extent and under certain conditions affected by their reproductive status, with physical danger and an uncertainty of return being greater constraints than physical strength and child care compatibil-ity (Peacock 1991, 350–58). There are, however, no agricultural tasks that cannot be undertaken by both women and men, and the variations among farming societies as to the nature of gendered work are considerable. In-deed, with increasing male migration, gender differences in agricultural production have blurred.

In each of the following chapters, the gender division of labor is used as an analytical tool to investigate the current varieties of work, management, and property interests of women and men in the Third World. In this way, women are viewed as active producers and decision makers, essential par-ticipants in designing and determining agricultural change.

THE AGRICULTURAL LABOR FORCE

Since the late 1970s there has been considerable reevaluation of the data on gender roles in agricultural production, as well as the importance of women's role in domestic household production and maintenance. From this reevaluation, two key findings have emerged: (1) throughout the world, women's work and contributions to the economy are underestimated; and (2) the Western economic concept of the household as a "firm" can mask differing economic interests of men and women. Increasingly, from the community to the international level, development planners realize that in order to carry out equitable and sustainable development, these findings must be viewed as critical elements in examining the gender division of labor in agricultural systems.

International Labour Office reports estimate that women constitute 46 percent of the agricultural labor force in Africa, 45 percent in Asia, 31 percent in North Africa and the Middle East, and 40 percent in the Caribbean (Dixon 1982). Dixon (1983) cites sources that estimate that up to 18 percent of the agricultural labor force in Latin America is made up of women. Labor estimates often are based on insufficient, incomplete, or inaccurate data, and women are generally underenumerated.

Measuring Women's Agricultural Labor

When women are not counted as workers, development programs easily neglect women's specific economic interests. Underenumeration of women in the agricultural labor force is common and is related to women's invisibility in the cash cropping, land owning, and wage earning economy (Brydon 1989; Dixon 1982; Safilios-Rothschild 1994; Whitehead 1994).

Many difficulties occur in attempting to measure the flexible and sporadic work patterns associated with shifting economic and seasonal farming demands. In Third World nations, women and men tend to be employed on only a part-time basis. Moreover, the line between domestic labor for consumption and economic production for sale or exchange is not clearly drawn, encouraging extension workers and researchers to define women's work as domestic—that is, not productive and not important to economic development.

Certain approaches to gathering agricultural labor data do lead to the inclusion of women's work in official estimates of the agricultural labor force, however (Anker 1994; Dixon-Mueller 1985; Whitehead 1994). As discussed by Dixon (1982), these approaches are: (1) to include subsistence

agricultural production with commercial agricultural labor; (2) to enu-
merate unpaid labor or participation in labor networks; (3) to consider
women's activities such as household food processing, storage and transport, small animal and poultry care, and kitchen gardening as economically
active or domestic labor; (4) to specify a low minimum number of hours of
work as a criterion for inclusion in the labor force; (5) to stipulate a longer
rather than a shorter reference period for economically productive activities; (6) to collect data during a time of peak agricultural activity, when
women are most likely to be involved; (7) to ask women about both primary and secondary work activities; (8) to base specific questions regarding
wage and nonwage work on information on women's agricultural work
patterns in the region; (9) to ask women directly about their work rather
than asking men, who may have culturally influenced reasons for discount-
ing women's work; and (10) to include the agricultural work of girls and
boys between ages 10 and 15 in data collection.

A farm-level data collection framework should analyze productive activities in the areas of subsistence and cash cropping as well as work in domestic household production. A key factor in gathering data on women is
team training in gender analysis at all points in the construction of a questionnaire. Critical also are clarifying the definition of the term *household
head* to include acting heads, interviewing household members in terms of
management units within the household (when appropriate), and gathering income allocation data on all earners in the household, including absent household members. Information on people who are not household
members but who contribute to or are recipients of household allocations
should also be gathered (Finan et al. 1991; Rogers 1990).

Direct observation and sample surveys provide estimates on the amount
of time individual members of a household spend in agricultural activity
directed to both subsistence and cash cropping. For a quick survey, a Rapid
Rural Appraisal with separate focused consultation groups of women and
men representing class, caste, and ethnic group diversity provides general
answers on the gender division of labor by task (Dixon 1985; Scrimshaw
1990). Dixon (1985) has suggested that researchers can obtain a form of
quantitative data by converting ethnographic descriptions of the gender
division of labor into rough estimates of proportions of labor contributed
to each crop or task by men and women. A more formal survey would
sample the population statistically and might produce greater variation in
responses but would also require more time.

Development planners and scholars increasingly recognize that in many
regions of the world, women and men are responsible for different crops

and often specialize in different aspects of agricultural production (Burfisher and Horenstein 1985; Guyer 1980; Mencher 1993; Momsen 1991; Pankhurst 1992). Moreover, the gender division of labor in farming systems has changed, and contemporary configurations do not necessarily reflect historical patterns. Guyer (1991:261) notes that in Africa, for example, "none of the old staples was monopolized by female labor"; instead, these crop production systems relied on activity-specific cooperative work. The present increased degree of crop-specific farming by sex in Africa relates to the introduction of New World crops beginning in the sixteenth century and colonial and postcolonial agricultural policies that drew men away from traditional subsistence farming.

Any analysis of complex contemporary farming activities must deal with gender differences in agricultural work, with specific attention applied to tasks and the control of resources, as well as the various cycles of production and their relationship to time and space (Anderson 1992; Burfisher and Horenstein 1985; Cloud 1985). In many areas of Africa, a common task separation is for men to prepare the fields and women to weed them. Among the Tiv in Nigeria, women retain the income from yams while men retain the income from the sale of millet and rice (Burfisher and Horenstein 1985). In India, Mencher found varying divisions of labor by task in her study areas and regional variation in explaining the divisions, based on religious beliefs and other cultural traditions (Mencher 1993).

Labor profiles, representing seasonal labor tasks (such as preparing fields, planting, weeding, harvesting, storing, and processing) and estimates of person-days per month allocated to each task during an average farming season, indicate which crops demand specific efforts throughout the year. Such profiles show changes in the farming cycle and labor allocation with newly introduced crops or techniques (see Burfisher and Horenstein 1985).

Agricultural labor shortages frequently affect women more adversely than men, since women generally have less cash and less political influence to recruit a work party or request the assistance of junior males (Guyer 1984). When a shortage of labor occurs, women may decide to plant crops, such as cassava, that require less weeding and that can be harvested as needed, rather than the traditional crops, which are higher in protein but which may be more labor-intensive (Barnes 1984).

As farming becomes more integrated into the world market system, women often take on tasks traditionally assigned to men (Flora and Santos 1986; Ishak et al. 1985), but men do not commonly assume the tasks of women in regard to household duties (Flora and Santos 1986; Judd 1994). Therefore women may take on new agricultural tasks while continuing to carry out their previous household schedule. Many of the sources cited above contain specific suggestions for improving data collection and analysis of this process (see also Adepoju and Oppong 1994; Feldstein and Jiggins 1994; Ford et al. 1992; Moser 1993; Ostergaard 1992; Rao, Anderson, and Overholt 1991; Young 1993).

THE FARM HOUSEHOLD

In order to understand the nature of the gender division of labor within agricultural systems, it is necessary to investigate the strategies that members of a household use to manage available resources. To this end, researchers need to focus on gender differences in the allocation and control of farm resources and to work actively with policy makers to ensure that new information is incorporated into development planning. Indeed, giving attention to apparently nondominant household members' income-generating and subsistence agricultural work and strategies helps to focus development planning and assistance on the people who do much of the work and who make many of the farming decisions (Adepoju and Oppong 1994; Blumberg 1992; Bruce and Dwyer 1988; Gladwin 1993; Momsen 1991; Netting 1993; Rogers 1990; Safilios-Rothschild 1994).

Household Work Patterns

Although women's participation in agriculture varies throughout the Third World, women do engage in clearly defined agricultural field work. Often they work in selecting seeds, weeding, organizing labor exchanges, and providing food to farm workers (Momsen 1991; Stead 1991). To identify female labor patterns, development planners also need to look beyond who is working in the fields and pay attention to related work, such as gardening, raising small livestock, and making handicrafts—activities that are important to the survival of rural households. As Flora and Santos have noted for the Dominican Republic, "the better off peasant households are households with multiple survival strategies based on female activity" (1986: 221). When planners recognize the importance of women's farm work, they can design more effective project components. In the Dominican Republic again, when household gardens were incorporated into project planning, women eagerly adopted them, and gardens were quickly initiated by more than 6,000 households (Flora and Santos 1986).

Women's house and yard activities were a significant factor in the "productivity of rural labor accompanying the cash crop revolution of the late nineteenth and early twentieth centuries" (Richards 1983:21), and they continue to be of great importance. Research has shown that such activities, which are performed mainly by women, may take up as much time as farming and marketing (Lagemann 1977 and Spiro 1980b, cited in Richards 1983:9). These activities may be invisible to researchers, especially in the case of male researchers investigating agricultural and household labor in areas where tradition prohibits conversation between unrelated men and women or where women are secluded (El-Ghonemy 1993).

In Northern Nigeria, an increase in the seclusion of women coincided with the expansion of groundnut production for export. While groundnut production provided more household wealth, it also required that one-third of all compound labor, primarily women's labor, be devoted to shelling groundnuts (Richards 1983). These findings support Burton and White (1984), who argue that in systems using intensive techniques for cereal production, men's field work may rise relative to that of women, but women will increase the time they spend in processing the cereal crops, obtaining fuel and water, and providing child care (see also Ember 1983).

HOUSEHOLD MANAGEMENT

Many projects have concentrated on the "male head of household," assuming that he would distribute development benefits within the household unit (Bruce and Dwyer 1988:17). Within the past decade, studies have shown not only that individuals within a household make decisions to maximize their individual goals but also that these goals may even be antithetical to those proclaimed for the household as a unified entity or "firm" by researchers applying a classic Western household model (Benería and Roldán 1987; Rogers 1990; Tinker 1990; Young 1992).

Within and between households, individuals use economic strategies to maximize their goals. These may not be the goals of a household unit but rather of individuals within the household. In fact, women and men may conceal income from one another and make investments outside the household, as when a woman leaves livestock with a member of her natal family in order to maintain control of it. Household members may also deliberately invest in an object (such as a sewing machine) that the other spouse will not want or use (Reynolds 1982).

The assumption that the household head controls the labor of all the household members often proves unfounded (Guyer 1980; Momsen 1991). West African husbands and wives, for example, seldom form a unified production unit (Hill 1972); households in highland Peru are the site of conflict, negotiation, and power struggles (Deere 1990); and on Montserrat, in the eastern Caribbean, relations within households are closely linked to uses of space, with women creating and controlling houseyards, where economic and social reproduction take place (Pulsipher 1993). Households often have more than one economic decision maker, and decisions may be based on relations with kin and non-kin, who may or may not reside in the same household (Pankhurst 1992).

Extra-household resources and social support networks are often critically important to female household members but are unseen or undervalued by international development agencies. Indeed, goods and services may be transferred to individuals who are not within the residential household or to other highly mobile individuals, and income allocations and obligations often extend beyond the household. Where polygyny or serial monogamy are prevalent, the income allocation priorities of male and female household members may conflict (Dwyer 1983; Scrimshaw 1990).

Just as benefits from development programs may accrue to one household member more than to others, household members who benefit only marginally from such programs may be asked to support, through their labor, economic activities from which they do not expect much reward (Rogers 1990). In some areas, such as northern Cameroon and The Gambia, women farmers are rejecting this situation and demanding more economic compensation from their husbands than previously (Carney and Watts 1991; Jones 1982).

A number of studies have indicated that women's access to and control of resources are critical to children's nutrition (Bennett 1983; Blumberg 1989; Dwyer 1983; Kumar 1978). Data from the Philippines suggest that increases in a woman's estimated wage income positively affect her own and her children's share of household food resources (Senauer 1990). As Dwyer (1983) and Bruce and Dwyer (1988) have observed, women's allocation priorities often focus on survival strategies for themselves and their children, while men's priorities often focus on mobility.

The Woman-Managed Household

The woman-managed household is a growing phenomenon in both the developing and the developed world (comprising more than 20 percent of all households), and one closely linked to poverty. In the Third World, Latin America and the Caribbean have the highest proportions of women-headed households, followed by Africa, with Asia having the lowest (UN 1991:17–18).

Among women-headed households, traditional gender expectations cannot be easily fulfilled. In Lesotho, for example, about half the men are absent from the country at any given time (Adepoju 1994:32). Similarly, in the eastern Caribbean 35 percent of all households are headed by women (Momsen 1993a:5). Frequently, however, female farmers in female-managed households are not viewed as independent farmers but are considered to be supported by remittances or other resident family members. Senior household members may even claim that the women are not making significant decisions and do not need additional assistance.

To clarify such issues, and to identify areas where help is needed, researchers (Youssef and Helter 1983:232) defined two categories of women-headed households: *de jure,* in which no male spouse or partner is present (i.e., the woman is divorced, widowed, or single and supports the family), and *de facto,* in which the male household member is temporarily absent but may send remittances, or in which the male is present but his economic contribution to the household is minimal (for more recent works, see Evans 1992 and Gladwin 1993).

Because of labor shortages, a lack of access to political resources, and cultural and religious proscriptions, women-headed households are often severely disadvantaged. A major strategy for women is to attach themselves to larger households. The result, as indicated in a survey in Chad, is that more widows and divorced women may be part of male-headed households than form independent units (Finan et al. 1991).

Women-headed households are characterized by smaller crop acreage planted, fewer oxen, lower agricultural output, and a higher proportion of production needed for family consumption. They also more often lack credit or income to pay laborers or buy more efficient technologies and are less frequently contacted by extension agents. In contrast to women in jointly headed households, women-headed households in Africa may specialize in certain income-generating activities such as making beer, selling produce and crafts, or performing off-farm labor. Because they consume most of what they produce, women-headed households have not benefited very much from higher farm produce prices generated by some structural adjustment policies (Due 1991).

Appropriate foci of data collection in any development program are the gender-related patterns of household consumption, the nature of the labor force, the control of resources, land allocation, types of reciprocal labor, time budgeting, labor constraints, and access to inputs, including credit and training. Planners need to work directly with rural women and men. It is only through enlisting people's participation in providing both general and specific information on the nature of the gender division of labor in agricultural field and garden work, and in domestic maintenance activities, both in male-headed households and in *de facto* and *de jure* female-headed households, that effective farming systems interventions can be designed.

At a time of changing perspectives on the gender division of labor, women's groups can come together to articulate their own development agendas and can be a means of modifying traditional perceptions of self-interest to include more equal roles for women in the household as well as in the community (see Papanek 1990:180–81). Such groups, however, frequently suffer from having a weak financial and management base. Women-headed households, which can benefit from membership in such community groups, are often the least likely to have the time or resources to participate (Finan et al. 1991).

2

TIME ALLOCATION

Judith Warner

Time allocation surveys complement research on the gender division of labor, documenting the economic strategies of women and indicating periods of actual or probable excessive labor demand, or labor bottlenecks. As Wollenberg (1988:128) notes, "the roles of women, children and the aged are often overlooked or discounted because the analysis focused on income generation or male 'heads of households.'" Daily schedules of women's expenditures of time provide a gauge for establishing the relative need for women's household or subsistence crop labor. Such schedules also provide data on areas where women may be reducing time spent on crops for family consumption or economic benefit and concentrating on cash crops, the income from which is often managed by men. Dixon-Mueller and Anker (1988) suggest that planners can use time allocation surveys to determine the seasonality of over- or underemployment for women agricultural wage laborers. Similarly, local-level planners can conduct time allocation surveys before and after the introduction of project interventions in order to determine their effect on women's workloads and identify ways to free women's time for project-related activities (McSweeney 1979a).

Time allocation surveys measure the time women spend on economic activities related to subsistence and income generation and on domestic household activities. Dixon-Mueller and Anker (1988:43) identify the three most commonly used general activity categories as: (1) economic activities, including market work, market-oriented production, and subsistence-based economic production; (2) housework and child care, including domestic work, household maintenance, and child care; and (3) nonwork (including leisure, recreation, eating, resting, personal maintenance, and visiting).

McSweeney's (1979a) research in Burkina Faso is an example of a comprehensive time allocation survey. Her categories of analysis include production, supply, and distribution; crafts and other professions; community; household; personal needs; and free time. She further breaks the "production, supply, and distribution" category into subcategories: food and cash crop production, domestic food storage, food processing, animal husbandry, marketing, brewing, water supply, and fuel supply. According to this categorical scheme, women in a village in Burkina Faso spend most of their time on work related to agriculture. Women spend an average of 367 minutes per day on food production, supply, and distribution, in contrast to 202 minutes expended by men (McSweeney 1979a:381).

More recently, in a study on resource management in the Philippines, Buenavista and Flora (1994:39) used the following categories: agricultural production, livestock production, fruit production, vegetable production, social reproduction, coastal/aquatic activities, attendance at meetings, off-farm activities, and nonfarm activities. They constructed a calendar to show seasonal changes in production, the period called the hungry months, seasonal changes in cash flow, and the seasonal incidence of illness.

The studies cited above provide sets of survey categories that can be used to generate information for development planning. Feldstein and Jiggins 1994, Engberg, Sabry, and Beckerson 1988, Wollenberg 1988, and Acharya and Bennett 1981 contain examples of other approaches to determining how women and households prioritize and allocate time for necessary activities.

METHODS FOR COLLECTING DATA ON TIME ALLOCATION

The methods most often used for collecting time allocation data include direct observation, time-use recall, and informant record keeping. Each method has its advantages and disadvantages.

Direct Observation

For this method, the researcher spends considerable time watching village women and is therefore usually restricted to relatively small samples (Johnson 1990). Using random observations, or spot checks, of women's activities allows a larger sample to be studied and may help minimize bias in the methodology (Acharya and Bennett 1981; Colfer 1994; Dixon-Mueller

and Anker 1988; Wollenberg 1988). For purposes of simplification, researchers often note direct observations on a preconstructed activity list.
Such a list must be carefully prepared to account for difficulties in defining
particular activities, determining when one activity stops and another be-
gins, and classifying two or more activities performed simultaneously.
Young (1993:111) notes that a woman hauling water to her house is doing
"unproductive" work that is likely to be ignored in time-use surveys,
whereas her husband working on a project to lay water pipe to the village
is doing "productive" work that is more readily counted by observers.

Activities carried out in groups and interruptions in activities are also
difficult to classify, and the presence of the observer or interviewer can bias
research results (Johnson 1990; Wollenberg 1988). Peluso (1979) writes that,
with time and patience, women may become used to the presence of the
observer, thus minimizing bias in the research.

Time-Use Recall

Researchers can also determine women's time-use patterns through interviews based on respondent recall, a less expensive and more efficient
method than direct observation (Dixon-Mueller 1985; Johnson 1990).
Either sequential recall or activity-specific recall can be used. The former is
based on respondent recall of an entire day's activities in the sequence in
which they occurred, while activity-specific analysis involves going over a
list of activities, with the respondent estimating the amount of time spent
on each. The reliability of the time-use recall method varies with the
length of the reference period, whether day, month, year, or season (Dixon-
Mueller and Anker 1988; Wollenberg 1994), with the shortest time lapse resulting in the most reliable responses (Johnson 1990). Zeitlin (1990:158)
notes that "recall captures the passage of time as people remember it, or, in
other words, framed in the mental constructs that people use in planning
and evaluating the use of time as a resource."

Wigna, Suryanata, and White (1980, cited in Dixon-Mueller and Anker
1988) indicate that monthly estimates of labor for an Indonesian time survey averaged 60 to 70 percent of daily observations. They concluded that if
the monthly estimates of hours spent on tasks are used to obtain proportions rather than absolute figures, measurement errors are not significant.

Interviewers can improve the reliability of time recall by cross-checking
respondent answers with other individuals or by direct observation. Precise
estimates of hours and minutes may not always be necessary. For example,
Anker, Khan, and Gupta (1987, cited in Dixon-Mueller and Anker 1988)
asked respondents about the length of time they spent on the tasks on a list

of 15 activities. The categories included, for example, "a small amount of time" and "a full day" to estimate hours, and "throughout the season" and "rarely or occasionally" to estimate frequency. The researchers then translated the rough estimates into hours and days, which they considered accurate enough to describe labor profiles for the people of the study area.

Informant Record Keeping

This method requires participants to keep detailed records of their activities and has seldom been used for research on Third World women because it requires either literacy or another person reporting on the woman's activities. A creative response to this problem was developed by Mencher, Saradamoni, and Panicker (1979) and Saradamoni (1991), who devised a visual time schedule in which women checked off pictures of what they were doing on a time sheet that had a rising sun to designate each day. Another innovative data gathering technique was created by Leesberg and Valencia Chavez (1994), who invented a game of drawings representing type of work, worker, and time spent. The visual game was interesting and fun to the families in rural Colombia who participated in the study. The authors determined that the data gathered were accurate and representative by cross-checking them with interviews, case studies, and other measurements.

Dixon-Mueller (1985:42) notes that all time-use surveys are complicated by the "ambiguous, blended or multi-layered" quality of real-life activities. Some women's activities, such as caring for children, usually occur simultaneously with the performance of other activities. Nevertheless, time-use surveys provide vital information about women's activities that cannot always be determined by a quick village visit or limited conversations with women. Rapid Rural Appraisal methods combined with more in-depth survey methods also can be effective means of gathering information on women (Suphanchaimat 1994). To examine women's use of local resources, Rocheleau et al. (1989) used group discussions, opportunistic interviews in the field, household interviews, and discussions with local experts and specialists. They recommend using Rapid Rural Appraisal methods followed by other data gathering techniques in order to acquire as much information as possible.

SEASONALITY AND TIME ALLOCATION

Time allocation studies can help determine seasonal peaks in men's and women's workloads. While all members of farming households face changes in demand for labor and other seasonal stresses, some problems are specific to women—for instance, childbearing and absence of males because of their migration for work. Female household members face unexpected increases in workloads if men return late or not at all from seasonal migration (Gill 1991). While contributions from all household members are important during times of seasonal stress, necessary seasonal adjustments often seem to fall disproportionately on women (Agarwal 1992b:189–90).

Delgado (1979a) studied men's and women's time allocation patterns during the rainy and dry seasons in two ethnic groups, the Mossi and the Bisa. He found that during the rainy season Mossi women, besides their regular duties, did a wide variety of tasks ordinarily considered to be men's work. At this peak time, Mossi women carried out 10 to 20 percent of many traditionally male activities such as watering crops, constructing fences, guarding fences or fields, and joining invitational labor groups. Indeed, Mossi women were so pressed for time during the rainy season that they reduced the time they spent on household tasks and crafts as much as possible. Other researchers have found that during the rainy season the women's energy output is higher than their energy intake (Bleiburg et al. 1980). Bisa women had lower rates of labor participation in traditionally male tasks, though they did the majority of fence construction work during the rainy season. In both groups, women's agricultural workloads dropped off during the dry season, although they often continued to harvest or transport crops (Delgado 1979a).

Delgado (1979b) also studied women's workload fluctuation by fortnight during the peak season. He found that women's time allocation for farm work varied in length during the demanding rainy season. In fortnight 1, women in a southeastern Burkina Faso village worked ten hours a day, while men toiled for nine. During fortnight 13, the groundnut harvesting season, women's farm work time expenditure dropped to seven hours, compared to five for men. In part, women's higher average time expenditure resulted from their need to continue household labor, although they sometimes abandoned time-consuming methods of meal preparation.

TIME ALLOCATION CONFLICTS

In regions where introduced cash crop production has increased, women's share of the workload has often been disproportionately affected (Agarwal 1992a; Burfisher and Horenstein 1985; Palmer 1979; Senauer 1990). In Nigeria, for example, an agricultural productivity project targeted input for the development of several cash crops among the Tiv (Burfisher and Horenstein 1985). Project personnel anticipated that the total workload would increase 14 percent on the typical small farm (2.5 hectares). The research showed, however, that while men's labor increased only 6 percent, women's increased 17 percent because of their greater responsibilities in harvest, post-harvest, and storage activities. Because of the seasonality of changing labor requirements, the increase posed difficulties for smallholder men as well as women. Women's increased time allocation for work on cash crops, which tend to be controlled by men, competed with the labor needs of their own crops. Men's labor input for the new crops became greater during periods when they were expected to contribute labor for women's traditional crops. In essence, the Tiv maintained a system in which men and women had the responsibility for separate crops but also contributed labor to each other's crops. The cash crop project disrupted this pattern by directing labor to crops controlled by men. As a result, labor bottlenecks developed among both men and women when new demands for work on cash crops conflicted with customary labor requirements for work on women's crops (Burfisher and Horenstein 1985).

Time allocation studies conducted before project inputs are selected can help pinpoint areas in which labor bottlenecks may occur and document possible conflicts between cash cropping and subsistence farming. They may also highlight the varying economic strategies of women and men. When demands on their time increase, women adjust the time allocated to certain activities in order to accomplish necessary tasks. As Moser (1993:72) states: "The fact that paid work and unpaid work are competing for women's time has important impacts on children, on women themselves and on the disintegration of the household." When planners use information regarding women's time use and allocation, development projects become both more realistic and more effective.

3

ACCESS TO LAND

Catherine Besteman

A crucial component of women's agricultural involvement—access to land—is obtained and maintained according to varying customs throughout the world. While women make up the majority of subsistence farmers, they have title to only 1 percent of the land (Dankelman and Davidson 1988:8–9). Rights to land—whether rights of ownership, control, or use—may be established by indigenous local land tenure practices, by law, or by particular agricultural projects. An understanding of women's rights of access to, use of, and control over land is critical in the development process to ensure that they continue to hold these rights in the face of planned change. Women's incentive and ability to participate in development projects, and the projects' potential advantages and disadvantages, depend on how their access to land is ensured. Therefore, understanding how and under whose authority land is apportioned within the community and the household is vital to understanding women's roles in agriculture. Agricultural projects planned without a full understanding of women's local access to land have frequently overlooked, ignored, or discouraged their very important role in agriculture.

ACCESS PATTERNS

Women may hold rights over land independently of men through inheritance, purchase, or usufruct from local authorities, yet even where they hold such rights, they may not retain management rights to it. In rural Tahiti, for example, men are owners of gardens and fields planted on land owned by their wives, and women do not control income from the sale of their husbands' produce (Lockwood 1993:153). In areas where women do not hold independent rights, they may receive rights of access to land through marriage or through informal methods such as borrowing. Where laws have mandated the privatization and adjudication of land, women have received variable rights to land and have often lost rights they formerly held under indigenous systems of land tenure (Akeroyd 1991). Similarly, development projects have often altered women's land tenure rights by installing new systems for acquiring and controlling land. Demand for land may increase when agricultural production becomes profitable as a result of such projects, resulting in pressure that may force poor farmers off their land (White 1992). Because women are often among the poorest farmers, the impact of development projects on their access to land must be carefully analyzed. Rights of inheritance and usufruct, and changes brought about through land privatization by national governments or development projects, are discussed in this chapter.

Inheritance

Inheritance patterns may give women full, limited, or no authority over land. In Java, Indonesia, for example, women and men have equal rights to inheritance and are treated equally with respect to property in marriage and at divorce (UNDP 1980). In Mutira, in Central Province, Kenya, while women may legally inherit land, it is still the male farmers' practice to pass land on to their sons (Davison 1988b). In some areas, such as Tunisia, women may have the right to own land in their own names but may not have full authority over it in practice (Jones 1981). Acting as a guardian, a brother or brother-in-law may control the woman's land, as is the case in other Muslim societies (Bernal 1988; Hahn 1984; Young 1992). In Bangladesh, although women can inherit land, "social factors and family politics inhibit women from claiming their formal rights" (White 1992:53). In those Latin American countries where women can legally inherit land, they may lose control of it to male relatives because of a general ignorance of the law. In some Latin American countries, such as Brazil, Bolivia, and Peru, married women are prohibited from holding title to land in their own names, making control of the land and access to credit difficult (Lycette and White 1989).

In some areas, complex customary tenure practices may obscure women's right to hold land. Among the Ehing of Senegal, for example, rights to land are held by patrilineages. Women move into their husband's patrilineal territory at marriage but maintain rights to land from a woman's natal lineage. Land from her natal lineage passes to her daughter, and upon the daughter's death it passes back to the women of the mother's natal lineage. So, while land is held by the patrilineage, some of this land circulates over generations only to its women (Schloss 1988).

Islamic law dictates that daughters are to inherit half as much as sons. In societies where Islamic law is in force, therefore, fieldwork is needed to determine whether women do indeed receive land in inheritance, and if so, who retains management rights. In a study in western Malaysia, researchers found that, while women inherit property, the state registers land titles in the names of men, leaving women without control of their inheritance. In addition, as land prices rise, only farmers with access to credit—usually the men who hold title—can buy land, so women are left with even less access to or control of property than before (Ng 1991).

Usufruct Rights

Many areas of Africa are characterized by clan or lineage trusteeship of land, although these traditional systems may be rapidly changing as a result of privatization. Under these systems, use rights to land may be inherited or may be determined by clan or lineage elders or a council. Women in these systems may or may not be able to inherit use rights or acquire them independently through the local authorities. Because of this variability, planners need to determine how and by whom use rights to land are acquired in an area. If women have independent access to lineage land, it is important to determine how the amount of land women receive compares with the amount of land men receive. Women's managerial rights to their land must also be investigated.

In many areas of the world, women have traditionally had independent access to farmland. Women in the coastal Sherbo area of Sierra Leone, for example, have high social status. They head the majority of residential compounds in the villages, and they can control the factors of production. Land is controlled by cognatic descent groups, and individuals—both men and women—have usufruct rights to it but cannot buy or sell it. In short, all Sherbo women who want to farm have access to land by virtue of being members of their descent group, and they have proven themselves successful and enterprising farmers (MacCormack 1982).

In contrast are systems in which women acquire rights to land through marriage. In these systems, women are often granted use rights by their husbands to land owned or held in usufruct by the husband. In some areas, such as Somalia, a wife who believes her husband has not provided her with enough land may use this as grounds for divorce (Besteman 1991). Women who marry into villages outside of their natal areas may be completely dependent upon their husbands for access to land. Where women acquire use rights through marriage, their fields are usually recognized as women's fields. Women hold recognized usufruct rights and managerial rights to the land they farm, and they control any income they obtain from the sale of their produce (Palmer 1985). For example, women of central Burkina Faso traditionally do not inherit rights to land use. Instead they are allocated land by their husbands, which they work themselves. Additionally, women help their husbands in the communal fields, the products of which are controlled by the husband (Henderson, Warner, and Ferguson 1982; McMillan 1980).

In these patrilineal land systems, men may appear to be the primary farmers. Women, however, often have important derivative rights to land, may produce subsistence crops that are critical for the household on their allocated land, and may be highly involved in the market economy by producing crops for the market. As men benefit from extension services aimed at increasing production and income from cash crops, women may be required to work harder and longer as unpaid family laborers on their husband's fields, giving up their own food crops and important sources of income. Married women may become completely dependent on their husbands, particularly where resettlement schemes or migration have separated them from their natal families. The manipulation of customary tenure practices to the advantage of men over women may also occur in areas experiencing cash crop development or government-supported projects (Carney and Watts 1991).

Systems based on usufruct rights vary from one society to another. The distribution of land within descent groups and the ways in which women receive access rights are important factors in development planning. Planners must also be aware of the division of labor between men's, women's, and household fields, and the custom governing control of the produce and income from the land. It is especially important to understand the position of widows, divorced women, and unmarried women, who may be in jeopardy if they have weak ties to men who allocate land. Moreover, in areas where the divorce rate is high, women may have only tenuous access to land and consequently may choose to invest in portable sources of income, such as livestock, rather than in improvements for crop production.

PRIVATIZATION OF LAND

The privatization of land and the commercialization of agriculture may decrease women's access to land. Privatization can occur as the result of national or local socioeconomic changes and population growth, or as the result of a government policy. Land adjudication and registration as implemented by many governments have effectively awarded land to a rural elite. In Cameroon, for example, this decision-making elite is almost exclusively male and is currently consolidating land that is thereafter not available for subsistence farmers (Goheen 1991). In some parts of India, privatization has resulted in the concentration of village commons land in the hands of a few large landholders, and many women are adversely affected because they lose access to fuelwood, fodder, and water sources (Agarwal 1992a). Control of land by elites in Bangladesh results in increased competition among wage laborers from resource-poor households, lowered wages, and increased costs for sharecropping (McCarthy 1993: 337).

Under land reform in Chile, only male heads of households were included, and only they had the right of membership in the producer cooperatives, which provide credit and services. Only about 2 percent of the beneficiaries were women (Deere 1986), although an estimated 15 to 19 percent of Chilean households are headed by women (Hahn 1984). Under the traditional bilateral inheritance system, divorced, abandoned, or separated women still had access to land with which to support themselves, a provision missing from the land reform scheme (Deere 1986). When women were excluded from the land reform process, their ability to participate in cooperatives and to receive technical services, and therefore their productivity, was severely hampered.

Land adjudication and registration programs have usually excluded women, thus hindering them from gaining secure access to land. Land adjudication in Kenya, for example, has had negative effects on female agriculturalists: women's traditional usufruct and managerial rights and rights to the sale of produce were ignored in the land adjudication scheme designed and implemented by men, and women lacked legal recourse if they were denied access to land under the system of title registration (Haugerud 1983; MacKenzie 1985). Fortmann (1981) examined the effect of Tanzania's national agricultural policy on the nation's women and found that agricultural policies have reduced their income and their families' well-being. All land belongs to the nation, but commercialization has resulted in land shortages, and men tend to be the recipients of land rights.

To cite other areas, recent land reform policies in the Dominican Republic applied only to men, further excluding women from control of and access to land and opportunities for credit and other aid programs (Abreu 1989). While women benefited from land reform in Peru in 1969, they were allotted only half as much land as men received in spite of the fact that nearly 30 percent of rural households were headed by women (Bunch and Carrillo 1990:76). Land reform in rural northern China in the mid-1980s also allocated half the amount of land to women as to men even though women had long been actively involved in cotton production in the region (Judd 1994:27). Women gained access to land in Nicaragua as a result of the Sandinista land reforms of the 1980s but primarily through participation in agricultural cooperatives, where they accounted for only 11 percent of the members (FA–CIPRES 1992:31).

Where land titles are awarded only to men, women effectively lose all rights to the land they farm; men are able to sell or rent land without the permission of the woman who might be farming it (Palmer 1985). Among the Luo of Kenya, for example, women are actively involved in agricultural production, but they have been excluded from holding title to the land they work. Men have the legal title, and therefore have collateral to obtain credit, which women lack (Stamp 1990). In Kenya, as in many areas of the world, having title to land is crucial for receiving access to agricultural services; obtaining credit, loans, and technical assistance; and joining producer cooperatives. Hahn (1984:28–29) cites a study on Kenyan law which notes that "land registration dispossesses women of the security of tenure that they had in family holdings," thereby hampering their ability to produce effectively. Women's "lack of secure rights to land," she adds, "is a disincentive to increase production."

RESETTLEMENT

Programs involving resettlement have tended to ignore women's usufruct or inheritance rights to land, to favor men over women as primary farmers and recipients of aid, or to resettle families in project areas where only men receive and control land. The following examples demonstrate how resettlement projects may affect and transform women's land rights.

In Burkina Faso, the AVV (Autorité des Aménagements des Vallées des Volta) resettlement project attempted to move families from the overcrowded plateau to the sparsely settled river valleys in order to ease pressure on the land and increase agricultural production (McMillan 1980).

Under this project, land partitioned to each family was the official responsibility of the household head. Male and female farmers were not allocated fields, as they had been in their traditional village systems. Some women did receive separate fields partitioned from the family farm, but these fields amounted to less than half of what women had previously cultivated as private fields. Not surprisingly, women participants were dissatisfied.

In some project areas, women illegally cleared private plots outside the resettlement villages. Women who left the project villages because of a lack of access to resources frequently had lost access to land in their traditional villages as well. Women who stayed had to work harder, especially on their husband's fields, although the husband received the sole remuneration. Thus, women had lost their separate sources of income (McMillan 1980; Palmer 1985). In another AVV region, however, project women successfully modified aspects of early AVV policy. In recent years, the AVV has responded to women's stated needs by allocating land to them.

Under the Ilora Farm Settlement in Nigeria, land titles were granted only to male heads of households, on the assumption that the men would equitably organize family members. In the traditional system, women had independent access to land, and husbands and wives did not pool their incomes. As a result of the resettlement scheme granting titles only to men, women lost status and an independent access to income. Consequently, they were often the first household members to leave the resettlement area (Spiro 1985). In another example, land reform in Zimbabwe allotted land in resettlement areas to male household heads; women had access to the land only through their husbands (Pankhurst and Jacobs 1988). Even if resettlement is planned so that women are allocated land separately, controls must be in place to ensure that such land is equal in quality to that allocated to men.

WOMEN-HEADED HOUSEHOLDS

Whereas the position of married women is hampered by male-dominated land ownership, the situation of divorced, separated, or abandoned women is often much more difficult. Women head 25 to 35 percent of rural and urban households in much of tropical Africa (Due 1991:104), about one-third of households in the Caribbean (Momsen 1991:25), and nearly 30 percent in all of Latin America (UN 1991:18). If land title goes to men, or if only men are named as beneficiaries in land reform or agricultural development projects, the position of divorced, widowed, separated, or abandoned women becomes even more tenuous. Frequently these women have extremely limited or no access to land on which to produce food for themselves and their families, and possibly to garner income. In Africa, where women are the primary food producers, and, indeed, in all regions of the Third World, prohibiting or constraining women's access to land severely affects overall food production (Dankelman and Davidson 1988; Gladwin 1993; Henn 1983; Momsen 1991; Schoepf and Schoepf 1988). Women heads of households who have access to land but not to the resources necessary to work the land (such as time, family labor, or money to hire labor, animals, and other resources) may face insurmountable obstacles to production (Pankhurst and Jacobs 1988).

De facto women heads of households whose husbands have emigrated also face the constraints mentioned above if all the land is in their husband's name. Although the wife may be the primary farmer, she may be barred from joining cooperatives, participating in training programs, or obtaining credit because the land is not in her name (Akeroyd 1991). Relatives or clan members of the husband may retain managerial rights to the land or rights over the produce or income. The wife's incentive to increase production or modernize the farm may be reduced as a result. When women's access to services is restricted or cut off, their productivity and efficiency as farmers falls, as does their incentive to adopt new practices or to attempt to increase productivity.

The final point to be stressed is that women have proven abilities as farmers and farm managers even in the face of discrimination and restrictive laws and customs (Moock 1976; Staudt 1978). Henn (1983) compared the productivity of Tanzanian Haya women who were landowners with other Haya women who farmed but did not own their land. She found that the landowners, unlike the nonlandowning farmers, held impressive entrepreneurial and agricultural skills, had a higher standard of living, grew cash crops, and hired male laborers. As Henn argues, "the improvement and expansion of the traditional women's food sector is likely to be both the cheapest and most reliable method of increasing domestic food supply" (Henn 1983:1051). Providing and ensuring women's access to land is a crucial variable in this process.

Where women and men traditionally farm separate fields and even separate crops, restricting women's access reduces their productivity, their ability to provide for their families, and their chance of earning a separate income, as well as upsetting the balance that may have traditionally existed between men and women. Women's usufruct and inheritance rights must be acknowledged and included in development planning.

4

INCOME GENERATION

The three sections of this chapter represent three related but distinct means people pursue to generate income in the agricultural sector. Women are involved in cash cropping, marketing, and wage labor to varying degrees throughout the Third World, depending on culture, traditions, geographic location, changing economic structures, and other factors.

A. CASH CROPPING / Catherine Besteman

The commercialization and mechanization of agriculture, leading to increased production of cash crops, has had both positive and negative consequences for women of the Third World. The benefits lie primarily in enabling them to earn a cash income in an increasingly cash-based economy. Unfortunately, in many areas the negative consequences for women have been much more prevalent. The effects of cash cropping on women are analyzed below in three key categories: women's access to land, women's access to cash cropping, and competition for resources between food crops and cash crops.

Women's Access to Land for Cash Cropping

It is well documented that women often lose access to land when cash crops are introduced (Charlton 1984; Cloud 1984; Dankelman and Davidson 1988; ISIS 1984; Meena 1991; Rocheleau 1988; Shiva 1989). As more productive land is dedicated to cash crop production, which is often controlled by male farmers or by agribusinesses, women are left with less land

and with increasingly marginal land. In Africa, commercialization has been a major force in shifting land tenure systems from use rights on community land to the individualization and consolidation of land rights. In the process, women lose their traditional use rights (see Chap. 3; also Blumberg 1981; Shiva 1989). In Asia, increased commercialization by large plantations has led to a large class of landless women working as agricultural wage laborers (see Agricultural Wage Labor, this chap.). Similarly, in Latin America, large plantations have contributed to the process of proletarianization of the rural workforce (Deere 1990; Deere and Leon 1987). Land reform and resettlement schemes there have often had the same consequences for women as those in Africa. With the emphasis in these programs on cash crops for men, women either receive no land for their own crops or are left with only a small kitchen garden (Blumberg 1981). Where women do retain access to land, their choices of which crops to grow are often constrained since men make many of the decisions regarding agriculture.

Division of Labor

Labor and Time. A major constraint on women producing cash crops is the cultural perception of the division of labor. In much of Africa, women are considered responsible for feeding the family. Where wives and husbands keep separate fields, men have traditionally had more options for moving into cash cropping on their own fields and leaving the production of subsistence crops to their wives. With this increased responsibility, women often do not have adequate land, labor, and time to produce their own cash crops. Furthermore, they frequently work as unpaid family laborers in their husband's cash crop fields. Men, however, are not necessarily under any obligation to share the proceeds from their fields with their wives (Fortmann 1982; Hemmings-Gapihan 1982; Henn 1983; Kennedy and Cogill 1982). In Sri Lanka, for example, census data show that women are more likely than men to be unpaid family workers in agriculture and less likely than men to have an income in cash or kind (Dixon-Mueller and Anker 1988). In Burkina Faso, the traditional family farm pattern is to work collective fields over which the household head maintains control and from which the family is fed. Small fields of cash crops are managed and controlled by individual family members. Men spend more time than women in their cash crop fields and less time on the family subsistence fields. Women, in their traditional roles as providers of food for the family, fill the gap created as men turn to cash crops. Consequently, women devote the majority of their time to the family subsistence field, greatly reducing the time available to work in their own cash crop fields. Beyond this, women are expected to meet many of their personal and economic needs for the year from their own fields and are thus in a double bind: they have a greater need for cash in the increasingly monetized economy, yet their access to a means of earning it is reduced (Hemmings-Gapihan 1982).

Kofyar women in Nigeria are exceptions to the negative cases presented above, having always had control over their labor and income and having maintained it as their circumstances have changed in recent years. The Kofyar as a group have moved into cash cropping since the 1960s, and women have participated in the change, marketing their own produce and diversifying their sources of income. Both women and men grow yams as their primary cash crops and grains for subsistence. Women also raise livestock, brew beer for consumption and sale, and prepare food for sale (Stone 1988).

Research in the Caribbean indicates that small-scale cash crops are often mixed in with women's subsistence gardens (Barrow 1993; Berleant-Schiller and Maurer 1993; Brierley 1993; Pulsipher 1993) and that women generally control production, marketing, and the income from the crops. According to Barrow (1993:190), women's cash cropping and other income-generating activities are seen as a natural part of women's role in maintaining their households.

Access to Cash. Access to cash is another important constraint on women's production of cash crops and improvements in their yields of subsistence crops. If a woman does earn cash—from the sale of a surplus, for example—she often uses it for family needs such as school fees or better food. Her ability to save and invest in agriculture is constrained by other household demands as well. Women often do not have the financial resources to invest in inputs or labor-saving technology (Dankelman and Davidson 1988; Mosse 1993). In Tanzania, rising prices farmers receive for cash crops, particularly cotton, have not kept up with the rapidly rising costs of farm implements. This has particularly affected women, who receive little or no cash for food crops and therefore have limited access to cash for tools or fertilizer to increase production (Meena 1991).

Dey (1984) notes that in some areas men are responsible for purchasing inputs and technology. Sometimes they also plow and seed their wives' fields. Timing emerges as a problem in this case, especially when wives' fields are prepared last and suffer a decrease in yields due to the delay. The equipment and technology in which men may invest for their own fields may not be suitable for women's fields when different crops are introduced (Dey 1984; Spring 1988) or if cultural norms prevent women from driving tractors or plowing fields. The problem for women-headed households is even greater. With a shortage of male household labor, the cost of purchasing inputs and hiring male labor for male tasks is often prohibitive.

Information and Extension. Governments, extension personnel, and development project personnel have traditionally targeted men as recipients of resources and information on cash cropping. The assumption has been that men would share information with women or that women, as producers of subsistence crops, had no need for new and direct information. Cultural factors have also been important. The commercial farming in India that grew from the Green Revolution requires producers to be in contact with outside males, such as government officials and dealers in agricultural products—activities from which women are often excluded (Blumberg 1992; Shiva 1989; Spring 1988).

This kind of discrimination in disseminating information, discussed in more detail in Chapter 7, not only provides a barrier against women producing cash crops but also constrains their ability to increase their production of subsistence crops.

Subsistence Crops and Cash Crops

Charlton (1984:87) summarizes the negative consequences of cash cropping on women's farming:

> Third World countries have been drawn into the international trade in foodstuffs, and many governments actively encourage the production of crops that can be sold for badly needed foreign currencies. Women are most disadvantaged by this policy when they have no choice but to continue working in the subsistence economy—with crushing work burdens, few resources, and no institutional support.

In light of its potential impact on female and male work schedules and on food production in general, the desirability of encouraging cash crop production must be carefully investigated. Heavy emphasis on the production of nonfood or nonindigenous cash crops can place local populations in nutritional jeopardy by decreasing local crop diversity, increasing dependence on international market fluctuations, and shifting local consumption patterns (Frankenberger 1985; Garret and Espinosa 1988; Mosse 1993; Shiva 1989).

Worldwide, men are often in better positions to exploit new cash crops, and thus women have become increasingly responsible for food crop production (but see Safilios-Rothschild 1994 and Whitehead 1994). Changes in production strategies have resulted in increased work and decreased access to cash for women. Extension services and development projects should include new technologies, inputs, and extension information for subsistence crops. Increasing the yields of such crops, an important goal in its own right, will benefit women by providing them with a salable surplus. Food crops can also be cash crops on the domestic market. While not as attractive to governments because they do not supply foreign currency, such crops can be an important source of income for small producers and do not leave farmers at the mercy of world market fluctuations.

Structural adjustment policies (SAPs) have recently been implemented by the governments of many Third World countries, but SAPs designed to stimulate cash crop production benefit men more than women. Before establishing SAPs that encourage increased agricultural production, governments and development practitioners must ask "whether rural women are in fact *selling* food crops in a market or *buying* food crops to feed their families" (Gladwin 1991a:5). Women often have little access to the vital agricultural inputs necessary to increase production, so SAPs that focus on those factors without also focusing on making them more available to women will not benefit women directly and may serve to decrease food availability as prices rise and supplies diminish (Gladwin 1991a).

Programs to encourage cash crop production or to increase yields in food crops must be designed with women's needs as primary. The labor available to women farmers must be balanced against the labor requirements for the new crop. Women's access to the cash and credit needed to buy inputs to improve yields and access to such resources as land, water, and extension services must similarly be considered by project planners (Due 1991). Female farmers should not be compelled to increase their workloads in agriculture unless their direct benefits also increase.

B. MARKETING / Judith Warner

The nature and range of women's marketing activities are vital factors to consider in development planning. Throughout the world, women sell processed food, crops, and livestock for cash or barter (Berger 1989; Downing 1990; Jiggins 1984; Lycette and White 1989). In the Caribbean, Katzin's (1959) detailed study of the Jamaican country higgler (itinerant peddler) showed that marketing can involve high expenditures of energy and time for modest returns (Katzin 1959). The purchase of produce from individual neighbors, preparation (hand washing, bundling, and packing), travel to market, and selling are very time-consuming activities (see Besson 1993; Safa and Antrobus 1992). Time limitations generated by women's overall responsibilities and low level of resources are key constraints on their full integration into formal marketing structures.

Trinidadian women (McKay 1993) and Mayan women in Belize (Stavrakis and Marshall 1978) often confine their marketing to small-scale retailing of poultry, pigs, and goats or the excess produce of their gardens. In some cases, they miss out on the economic returns of formal markets; in other cases, women "prefer to sell produce [in informal markets] because it is 'what they know'" (McKay 1993:281). Talle (1988) reports that Masai women of Kenya market animal products, especially locally, on a small scale. Men control the marketing of animals, and a woman can only sell an animal in consultation with her husband, brother, or other male relative. Any livestock marketing scheme planned by the Masai, therefore, would be likely to overlook women, although plans for marketing livestock products such as milk and butter would be beneficial to women. Similarly, Due and Magayane (1990) point out that because women-headed households have less excess produce to sell, raising prices for farmers' produce will not benefit them. It may, in fact, raise their overall household costs.

Informal Markets and the Informal Sector

The definition of the formal economy as opposed to the informal is controversial. Several researchers have offered conceptualizations of the informal sector's relationship to gender analysis (see Antrobus 1992; Benería and Roldán 1987; Berger 1989; Mezzera 1989; and Tripp 1992). These authors criticize the dualistic juxtaposition of the formal and informal economies. They stress that the kind of work done by many women—i.e., small-scale, home-based, labor-intensive, low input and output labor—is an integral part of the so-called formal economy. In this section, the term *informal economy* refers to that "heterogeneous set of productive activities that share the common feature of employing a number of people who would be unable to find employment in the modern sector and must generate their own employment with relatively little access to the factors of production that complement the labor supply" (Mezzera 1989:47). While this definition is not perfect (it does not say how the "modern sector" is delineated, for example), it can at least serve as a framework for the discussion.

Blumberg (1989) notes several studies indicating that women's involvement in the informal sector is substantial, although it varies cross-culturally (Finlay 1989; Jiggins 1984; Singhanetra-Renard 1987). One study estimates that, worldwide, women comprise half or more of those active in the informal sector (Berger and Buvinic 1988, cited in Blumberg 1989). Safa and Antrobus (1992:64) note that in Jamaica 38 percent of women work in the informal sector, while in Nicaragua 60 percent of economically active women do so (Perez-Aleman 1992:245). Similarly, Berger (1989:12) refers to a study indicating that women own 60 percent of the small businesses and microenterprises in rural Honduras. The marketing of farm produce and by-products is an important source of income for women and is usually an informal sector activity.

Women's involvement in the informal sector can thus serve as a major mechanism for boosting local economic activities. Informal sector businesses often use local materials and products in labor-intensive activities, thereby stimulating local farming and employment. Informal markets in rural southern India, for example, provide a place for women who are producers to sell their vegetables, but most of the women vendors sell purchased goods or vegetables produced by other farmers. In an area with few employment opportunities, these markets offer rural women a means of earning an income, however modest (Singamma Sreenivasan Foundation 1993).

Women are active in local, low-profit-margin trading and are underrepresented in commercial ventures. Jiggins (1984) outlines the following factors as those responsible for women's greater involvement in informal marketing: (1) domestic and maternal responsibilities; (2) the autonomy possible in this type of marketing work; (3) a lack of equal access to higher-income marketing; and (4) a desire to protect their children during unstable times. Family responsibilities are a major factor restricting women's ability to participate in formal market structures. Local trading allows more flexible scheduling of time for travel to market and offers the possibility of child care assistance from local family members (Downing 1990; Jiggins 1984). Further, informal markets allow women to participate when they need to, which may be irregularly. Eviota (1992:130) notes that rural women in the Philippines may sell produce "when they need cash for a specific processed or manufactured item for their own consumption." Irregular participation in the market, however, results in low returns on produce for these women.

Women's involvement in informal marketing has a long tradition in some parts of the world. West African and Caribbean women, for example, are well known for their marketing skills and successes, and women in Central and South America, other parts of Africa, and Southeast Asia have also had a significant role in marketing (Blumberg 1989). Singhanetra-Renard (1987) reports that Thai women traders travel frequently in order to sell their produce at a regional market. Women from the area studied sold fresh produce and made daily trips to market. Male traders from the same village sold livestock and other items, traveling less often but for longer periods. The women are autonomous traders, adjusting their market schedule to reflect seasonal variations and family responsibilities. In some regions of Bangladesh, women sell goods in public markets as well as door-to-door, though such activities by women are not well accepted, and women traders only reluctantly introduce their daughters to them (World Bank 1990). White (1992) describes most women's participation in markets in Bangladesh as primarily behind-the-scenes, carried out through male intermediaries.

In the region of Lake Titicaca in highland Bolivia, Aymara women's increased access to Spanish-language education has facilitated their entry into the informal sector of the cash economy. Young Spanish-speaking women now sell craft items to a growing number of tourists in the area. The women also take advantage of travel to markets to socialize and to visit family members (Benton 1987, 1993). Meertens's study of households in lowland Colombia indicates that marketing activities are divided along gender lines, with women marketing eggs, dairy products, and domestic animals, and men buying and selling cattle and wood (Meertens 1993). White's study of the Ghanian production of gari (grated, toasted cassava flour) showed that once women had made initial capital investments, both farm producers of cassava and women employees of women's local businesses received increased incomes (White 1983). In Burkina Faso, women beer brewers raise capital and do their own processing, assisted by local women as employees. Those who are able to invest large amounts of time and capital accrue substantial profits (Saul 1981). At rural markets in the Philippines, women usually sell fruit, vegetables, and small plastic items, while men sell large fish, meat, and bulk cloth (Eviota 1992).

While informal market producers and traders enjoy flexibility and autonomy, they lack the protection that could be provided by government laws and policies. Often women work as traders in the informal sector because they have no access to other opportunities to earn an income and feed their families (Antrobus 1992).

Marketing Cooperatives

Women's cooperatives serve to strengthen women's roles in marketing. Women have created them to protect their earnings from husbands or male relatives and to deal with state regulations and harassment more effectively than they can as individuals (Blumberg 1989). Women have faced discrimination in dealing with state bureaucracies when they have sought to obtain licenses and permits, credit, and land rights (Blumberg 1989; McCall 1987). Because of cultural factors in some countries, men have been very suspicious of women's organizations and have introduced barriers to their success (Wilkinson 1987). Other difficulties women face in forming cooperatives include time constraints, which result in a high proportion of older women with fewer household obligations becoming participants, and internal social and economic conflicts, with more educated or wealthier members sometimes taking over and exploiting other group members (McCall 1987).

In a successful case from Korea, women established a cooperative consumer shop and a joint beef fattening venture (Jiggins 1984). They began by raising money for the shop by engaging in agricultural employment. Next, they adopted a rotating leadership system in which each woman headed the group for a month, thereby gaining management skills. In addition, community consumer needs that could be filled at the prevailing level of wholesale prices were assessed, thus guaranteeing a profit, and all the members pressed for the adoption of easily understood accounting procedures. These strategies ensured the success of the store. Later, women worked in teams of two to four to manage all phases of the beef fattening project, and they were able to secure livestock extension advice, sell cattle, and reinvest the profits. Important to the success of the project were community acceptance of the activity and the personal qualities of the woman leader of the group.

In western Nigeria, Yoruba women traditionally process and market food crops and control the profits from the sale of produce not consumed in the household. Ten Yoruba villages participated in a maize project that introduced a higher-yield variety of maize. The direction of flow of the maize and profits from its sale changed, as the higher-yield maize is used for animal feed instead of human consumption. It was sold by men's cooperatives formed to provide the male farmers better access to the inputs necessary for increased maize production. Eventually a new variety of high-yield maize for human consumption was introduced, and the women, who had been deprived of traditional benefits from maize production under the first project, formed their own cooperative to facilitate maize production and improve profits from trade. The women's cooperatives have grown as they have obtained loans and expanded their marketing activities (Ladipo 1991).

The Bangaray Gonzales Rural Women's club resulted from a visit to a village by a Regional Action Officer of the Philippine Ministry of Agrarian Reform. Development and group formation were discussed with village women. Under the leadership of a prominent local woman and working with a Regional Action Officer, the women established a cooperative to raise goats and to market vegetables and dried fish. The Agrarian Reform Extension Service presented a seminar on pre-cooperatives and capital to buy feed. The women's cooperative has generated enough profits to pay off the initial loan and to pay dividends to members. Instrumental in this project's success were the presence of a strong local woman leader and the structural support offered by the Ministry of Agrarian Reform (Jiggins 1984). Other examples of successful cooperatives formed by women in many parts of the world are found throughout this volume.

Transportation

Transportation is a critical factor affecting women's ability to participate in formal markets. In Bangladesh, for example, one study found that the cultivation of vegetables in areas of limited agricultural land was positively linked to the availability of a local market. Where a local market did not exist, only 6 percent of homestead space (the land immediately around the house) was cultivated, in contrast to 26 percent cultivated in areas with access to a local market (Chowdhury and Islam 1988, cited in World Bank 1990).

In the Caribbean, women farmers face many obstacles in taking their agricultural produce to local markets or commercial firms. Jamaican higglers harvest the produce of their neighbors and resell it through an arduous process of travel on foot or by bus or truck (Chaney 1983; Henshall 1981). Other women traders in the Caribbean travel outside their own regions to sell produce, and transporting themselves and their goods is a major aspect of their trading activities (Massiah 1993). Chaney (1983) observed that informal marketing methods and poor storage facilities result in post-harvest losses and nutritional deterioration of foodstuffs. Potential sales are also lost because women farmers who live far from market centers and who lack transportation cannot add the necessary travel to their other daily responsibilities (Henshall 1981). Thus, women traders' possible income from selling produce is limited to what they can earn through local sales.

In Tanzania, women and men formerly were responsible for transporting cotton and other crops to market for sale. However, in the past decade the cost of bicycles, wheelbarrows, and oxcarts to transport produce has risen beyond the means of most rural families. As transportation has become more expensive and limited, men have removed themselves from marketing, leaving women with increased responsibility for selling produce and greater demands on their time (Meena 1991).

Women have dealt with the problem of transportation in various ways. For example, the Revolutionary Ethiopian Women's Association, working with women's groups and the Food and Agriculture Organization of the United Nations, began a horticulture project in a refugee settlement. A hundred women worked together to plant vegetables on five hectares. Because they lacked transportation to reach other markets, they produced a variety of crops that they sold locally. While their sales have been limited as a result, the women report that the project has been valuable as a source of both income and food (Dankelman and Davidson 1988).

The Mraru Women's Group in Kenya, in contrast, has solved its transportation problem by gaining a means of transport. The group is affiliated with a national women's organization called Maendeleo ya Wanawake (Swahili for Women's Progress) (Kneerim 1980). At club meetings, women spoke of their transportation problems and decided to pool their funds to buy a bus. With additional support from outside personnel, including the guarantee of a loan by a social worker, the women were able to start a profitable trading and transportation business.

It is clear that planners who are considering marketing schemes designed to promote women's participation and increase their profits must take into account the larger context of women's lives—the time and labor constraints they face, their access to agricultural resources, their family and community ties and obligations, and the limitations on mobility they may confront. They must also be aware of the social role the market plays. Berleant-Schiller and Maurer (1993) describe markets in Dominica as settings for the spread of ideas and news. While at the markets, people send messages to other islands in the Caribbean, exchange political news, and renew and maintain friendships and family ties. Women producers and marketers play important roles in providing locally needed food and other goods, and at the same time marketing enables them to earn an income and to build and maintain ties with their communities (Safilios-Rothschild 1994). All these factors, in complex relationships with other aspects of women's lives, influence the outcome of any development project regarding marketing.

C. AGRICULTURAL WAGE LABOR / Elizabeth Howard-Powell

In response to economic pressures on landless and land-poor households in rural areas, women have sought employment as agricultural wage laborers in growing numbers, though with great regional variation in this trend in the Third World. In India between 1961 and 1981, the proportion of women employed in agriculture increased from 26 percent to 50 percent of economically active women (Agarwal 1988, cited in Shiva 1989:114). Women agricultural wage laborers in Brazil comprised 8 percent of economically active women in 1970, a figure that had risen to 33 percent by 1980 (Spindel 1987:55). In Mexico the percentage of women in the rural wage labor force rose from 2.8 percent in 1970 to 5.6 percent in 1975 (Arizpe and Botey 1987:79). Twenty-five percent of women in rural areas of Algeria were employed in agriculture in 1977 (Lazreg 1990:185). Finally, in Ghana in 1984, 56 percent of all employed women worked in agriculture or related occupations (Boateng 1994:99).

As the supply of female agricultural laborers has increased, in many areas the demand for their work has decreased, especially with increased mechanization, which tends to favor male labor (Dixon-Mueller and Anker 1988; Mitter 1994; Rassam and Tully 1988). Employment available to women is generally temporary and is typified by low wages, little job security, and poor working conditions. Men are often paid higher wages than women for the same job, and jobs done predominantly by women are paid less and have lower prestige than jobs predominantly performed by men. In spite of these disadvantages, women wage laborers in some areas outnumber their male counterparts (see, for example, Bardhan 1993 on India, Collins 1993 on Brazil, and Lockwood 1993 on Tahiti).

To integrate women's concerns into development efforts that could potentially affect agricultural wage labor patterns, factors underlying the varying extent and conditions of women's agricultural labor need to be recognized. These include technological change, labor organization, and cultural attitudes about women's work.

Technological Change

As agricultural production in recent decades has become more technology- and capital-intensive and less labor-intensive, many tasks previously done by laborers are becoming mechanized. Lower-class women have experienced the greatest loss of labor opportunities due to this transition, becoming concentrated in the lowest ranks of unskilled, temporary laborers who work primarily during peak agricultural seasons (Blumberg 1981; Sen 1982; Shiva 1989; World Bank 1991).

Java and Bangladesh provide examples of the contrasting impact that technological change has had on women's and men's opportunities for wage labor. Women traditionally were hired to do much of the labor in

rice farming, particularly the exacting and labor-intensive jobs of harvesting rice with small knives and of hulling the harvested rice. In recent
decades, the scythe (used mostly by male laborers) has been introduced for
rice harvesting, allowing one man to do the job of many women. In addition, rice hulling has been widely mechanized, displacing female laborers
who were highly dependent on agricultural employment. In rural Bangladesh, where hand hulling of rice was often the only source of women's
wage labor, mechanization has left women with few other sources of wages
(Cain 1981; Chakravarthy 1992; Stoler 1977; World Bank 1990).

In some instances, technological change can lead to increased employment. For example, Asian irrigation projects generate employment opportunities for male and female laborers, both in the construction of irrigation
systems and in increased agricultural production made possible through
irrigated farming (Silliman and Lenton, 1985). In Bangladesh the introduction of higher-yield varieties that require more fertilization has resulted in
increased labor needs and possibly more employment opportunities both
before and after the harvest (World Bank 1990). Unfortunately, as noted
above, women have been edged out of many of these opportunities.

Women's Labor Organizations

Women face particular problems in organizing to better their employment
opportunities and working conditions. Women's domestic responsibilities
and familial obligations curtail the amount of energy they can contribute
to organizational activity. In addition, traditions and norms may prohibit
women from coming together to form labor organizations. Arizpe and
Aranda (1981) note that young women may be particularly difficult to organize because they tend to be more docile and mobile than their older
counterparts. When threatened by fathers, husbands, or other male relatives, many women never attempt to secure wage labor, or leave it if it be-
gins to gravitate toward political activities (Stichter 1990). Rural women's
high rates of illiteracy and lack of political voice and power are additional
barriers to effective organization (Charlton 1984; Collins 1993). Female
migrant laborers face even more obstacles to joining or establishing labor
organizations because frequent moves for work inhibit the formation of
permanent groups at their place of work (Isikdag 1985).

In spite of barriers, women have successfully organized themselves into
government-recognized labor organizations. In Nicaragua, for example,
rural women are active in the Agricultural Workers Union. In 1985, 40 percent of the members were women, and more recently women held 35 per-

cent of its leadership positions. The union constructed 108 rural child care facilities in 1988 and 1989, and incorporated women's concerns into contract negotiations (Perez-Aleman 1992:250–51). In Kenya, women's groups hire themselves out to do wage labor on large farms or to work on government irrigation projects in exchange for extension services (Carloni and Horenstein 1986; Cloud 1985). Women's societies in The Gambia also hire themselves out for wage labor in order to increase income to the society. Such funds are used for the women's own fields (Norem et al. 1988). Despite their status as migrant laborers, women of the Transplanting Societies in Sri Lanka have successfully bargained for better pay and working conditions (Cloud 1985).

Cultural Attitudes Regarding Women's Work

Women's labor is undervalued, underreported, and underpaid. Women usually are viewed as being less productive than men, and they are paid less and receive only the least secure and least skilled jobs, which makes them easily replaceable by other laborers or by machinery. When employers assume that women are being cared for by men, women are the last to receive jobs, or they may see their wages given directly to their husbands (Charlton 1984; Dankelman and Davidson 1988; Dixon 1982; Mencher 1985; Shiva 1989).

In much of the Third World, women's reproductive roles are emphasized, while their productive activities remain invisible. While women's reproductive roles (particularly their role as the provider of food for the family) remain important, their access to resources such as land and labor to produce food has been diminished (Mazumdar and Sharma 1990; Trenchard 1987). The feminine ideal in South Asia and the Middle East is that women remain inside or at least near the home. Where economic pressures have forced them to seek agricultural wage labor, such work is viewed as a sign of low status by the community and by the women themselves (Sen 1982; Sharma 1984; World Bank 1991). In Algeria, severe economic conditions have pushed women into wage labor, but traditional views of women's proper roles have not changed concurrently. Women retain their household responsibilities at the same time that they perform wage labor outside the home (Lazreg 1990).

Young women in Mexico seeking work in strawberry packing plants were denounced by local priests and opposed by their fathers, who feared that the women would lose their morals if they worked outside the home (Arizpe and Aranda 1981). Stichter (1990) notes that, with time, men have come to accept women's employment as an economic necessity while continuing to restrict the types of work they consider acceptable for their female relatives. In India, manual labor is regarded as demeaning and not desired by women, who withdraw from wage labor as soon as their household economic circumstances allow (Ahmed-Ghosh 1993:194). The Indian women studied by Mencher (1993) who cease working in wage labor generally do not experience a decrease in the amount of work they do; rather, their household tasks increase as a result of larger harvests—the very prosperity that allowed them to leave the fields.

Women landowners may have problems on the other side of the wage labor issue. Barrow (1993) observes that women farmers on the island of Barbados have difficulty hiring laborers. Although they depend on seasonal wage laborers, they often cannot afford the high cost of temporary workers. In addition, male laborers consider working for women farmers to be low-status employment.

Economic crises in many parts of the Third World have thus resulted in many more women seeking and obtaining agricultural wage labor in order to survive. The type of employment available to them has been based on their traditional tasks in agriculture, but the need for cash income means that the definition of acceptable employment is expanding in many parts of the world (Dankelman and Davidson 1988; Mazumdar and Sharma 1990; Obbo 1990; Stamp 1990; Wickramasinghe 1993).

5

CREDIT

Catherine Besteman

Access to credit is critical for small businesses and the self-employed—the very sectors that experience the greatest difficulty in obtaining credit. Credit is necessary to expand production and distribution, to obtain new agricultural technology, and often just to maintain a business at a reasonable level of efficiency. Women are active economically—particularly in their roles as informal sector workers, traders, and agriculturalists—yet their access to credit is extremely limited. Poor women often have difficulty in applying for credit because of such institutional and structural factors as the limited dissemination of information about available credit, cultural biases that restrict women's access to credit, and women's lower levels of educational attainment and higher levels of illiteracy compared with men, especially in rural areas (Berger 1985, 1989; Carr 1991). The continued lack of access to credit means that discrimination acts doubly against women: as small business operators and as women.

Women and men often participate in different and separate economic activities in rural areas, especially where male out-migration is high. Many Third World women are largely or wholly responsible for the financial welfare of their families. For rural economic development to progress evenly, women must have equal access to credit, as well as to training and technical assistance. If credit is directed to families or households, women may be neglected because funds tend to remain with males (Moser 1993:50). The "trickle down" effect expected from rural credit programs targeted to male-dominated enterprises has not happened, especially where men and women are involved in separate productive activities (Berger 1989).

Throughout the Third World, women participate in informal networks to obtain credit and are members of organized rotating credit and loan associations (Berger 1989; Lycette and White 1989). Women also may borrow money from friends and relatives, or they make use of local moneylenders or pawn-brokers, usually at exorbitant interest rates (Lycette 1984; Lycette and White 1989; Reno 1981). The problems arising from women's use of these informal sources may include an accumulation of indebtedness and an exhaustion of the supply of money for loans. However, as Lycette and White (1989:33) point out, "although informal credit systems do not always provide sources and mechanisms necessary for the provision of credit to women, they do show that women use credit and suggest what features would be desirable and workable in a formal program intended to meet women's credit needs." Informal credit programs appeal to women because of their low transaction costs, immediate availability of funds, availability of small loans, flexible repayment arrangements, and minimal and flexible collateral requirements.

Where small-scale independent formal credit programs have been initiated, frequently the majority of borrowers are women. Lycette (1984:3) observed that the "high demand by women for credit in these community based programs provides at least indirect evidence that women have restricted access to credit in the formal financial system." While women continue to rely on informal networks to obtain credit, most development funds are available through formal sources, a situation which has important implications, "given the major role that women play in providing for the economic well-being of their families" (Lycette 1984:3).

Women face a number of obstacles in obtaining formal credit, especially through large institutions such as banks, cooperatives, and credit unions. These include the following:

Availability of Funds. When limited funds are available for loans, larger loans tend to be given to wealthier borrowers. Poorer borrowers seeking smaller loans are neglected. Women are often overlooked when "loan rationing" is practiced, and preference is given to wealthier farmers or businessmen (Howard-Merriam 1986; Safilios-Rothschild 1994).

Cultural Constraints. Because women need and want smaller loans, banks often perceive them as "riskier" clients (Lycette 1984). Misconceptions about women's ability to repay loans is another cultural factor limiting banks' willingness to lend to women (Reno 1981). A woman may need her husband's approval and signature in order to obtain a formal loan, but such approval may not be obtainable (Carr 1991).

Availability of Information. Women are often unaware of formal credit options and uninformed about formal loan procedures. In many areas, legal structures limit women's participation in cooperatives, which are often important sources of credit and credit information. In Kenya, for example, Staudt (1985) found that on the women-managed farms surveyed, 99 percent of women managers had no knowledge of the credit programs offered by the agricultural extension service in the area. Male extension agents generally deal with male farmers, limiting the amount of credit information available to women (Carr 1991). Illiteracy, which, as noted above, tends to be higher among women than men, is another major obstacle to information transfer, as the numerous forms necessary to apply for formal loans seem an insurmountable barrier (Berger 1985).

Transaction Costs. For rural women and men, travel to and from banks can consume many hours or even days. Women face greater constraints than do men in finding the money for travel expenses, loan service charges, and the bribes that are sometimes necessary. It is often more difficult for poor women than men to take time away from their families and domestic responsibilities to make the journey to the loan office.

Loan Size and Delays in Obtaining Funds. One reason women tend to prefer borrowing informally from friends and moneylenders is that they need small amounts immediately. Formal loan services often require loans larger than women want, and loan applications may take months to process.

Collateral. Requirements for collateral are a major obstacle for women interested in obtaining formal credit, especially in countries where women do not hold land in their own names. Land reforms in the Dominican Republic, Colombia, and Tanzania, for example, apply only to men, and women therefore do not have land to offer as collateral (Abreu 1989). In Brazil, Bolivia, and Peru, married women cannot own property in their own names and are thus denied personal access to credit (Lycette and White 1989:27). Land in Kenya is generally owned by men, and banks require a title deed and land as collateral for loans (Reno 1981). Because women's businesses tend to be in the informal sector (such as trading or marketing agricultural produce), their small operations generally cannot be used as collateral.

Repayment Schedules. Many studies have shown that it is easier for women to repay loans in frequent (sometimes daily) small installments rather than in the large, less-frequent payments generally required by formal lenders (see, for example, Lycette 1984; Otero 1987; Reichman 1989; and Russo et al. 1989). Women often prefer the credit arrangements of informal lending sources because they can use small amounts of money daily or weekly to repay loans

before the money is required for other purposes. Saving large amounts of
money to repay a loan is often very difficult for poor women who are responsible for the day-to-day welfare of their families and businesses.

SUCCESSFUL LOCAL CREDIT PROGRAMS

Credit programs aimed at the smallholder or small-business person achieve
greater success if they adopt some of the characteristics of women's indigenous
local credit arrangements. Rotating credit clubs in Nigeria, similar to those
popular with women throughout the world, provide one example (Okonjo
1979). Nigerian women are expected to make major contributions to family
financial needs and income. To help meet this need, women form rotating
local credit groups in which each member is expected to make contributions
to the general fund from which women take turns drawing loans. Nigerian
women studied by Okonjo used these local informal clubs in lieu of formal
savings-and-loan institutions because illiteracy and paperwork demands were
not a problem with the clubs. There were no collateral requirements or long
delays in receiving the loans, and frequent small payments were accepted.

Credit programs have changed and developed in some areas as development planners have come to realize that women continue to be excluded
(Berger 1985; Berger and Buvinic 1989; Duncan and Habib 1988; Jiggins 1984;
Lycette 1984; Otero 1987; White et al. 1986). The characteristics of successful
formal and informal credit systems that can serve as examples for development
planners are discussed in the literature cited above. They include the following:

1. Definitions of collateral include physical items such as jewelry and non-
   physical resources such as recommendations by leading community
   members and interviews with the women themselves.
2. Transaction costs of loan applications are lowered by assisting applicants
   in filling out the forms, reducing turnaround time, and locating loan officers in areas more accessible to rural women, perhaps by employing
   traveling loan officers.
3. Loans are made available in small amounts with flexible repayment practices, including the option of making frequent small installment payments.
4. Group lending is instituted, following the model of the rotating credit
   group.

The Integrated Rural Development Programme operated a project in
Bangladesh to make loans to women's organizations, which then made loans

to individual group members. Technical assistance accompanied the loans. The combination of small loans, no collateral requirements, group responsibility for repayment in case of individual default, and the incorporation of extension services resulted in women's work becoming more productive. The program had 25,000 members, and the default rate was almost zero (Buvinic, Sebstad, and Zeidenstein 1979).

The Nicaraguan Foundation for Development set up market women's co-operatives through which individuals could borrow. In lieu of collateral, loan guarantees were given by other co-op members, and repayment schedules were flexible. Women could make daily installment payments if they desired. Through this arrangement, women in the cooperatives learned to deal directly with banks, eventually becoming independent of the project (Buvinic, Sebstad, and Zeidenstein 1979).

In Malawi, the Women in Agricultural Development Project, funded by the Office of Women in Development of the U.S. Agency for International Development, met with success by reducing the size of credit packages, in the form of seeds and fertilizer, to the appropriate scale for smallholders. Whereas membership in male farmers' clubs and access to collateral had previously determined creditworthiness, women in this project were given access to credit through a verbal voucher by the village headman. Male extension workers were directed to contact women (see Chap. 7). Through these steps, the proportion of female credit recipients in the project went from 5 percent of the total to 20 percent in one year. All the women paid back their loans with money earned in household enterprises, such as beer brewing, and households became self-sufficient in food (Spring 1986).

INNOVATIVE FORMAL CREDIT MECHANISMS

In addition to combining technical assistance, extension, training, and credit, innovative methods that are not necessarily characteristic of the informal financial system can be highly effective in improving women's access to formal credit.

First, local leaders can be trained to evaluate loan applications, lend money, and help establish lending criteria for local communities. Manila Community Services, Inc. (MCSI) is a private voluntary organization in the Philippines, which set up the Self Employment Program using indigenous female community leaders as intermediaries. The intermediary loaned money locally, thus bringing the lending agency to the community. She required no collateral and worked out the terms of borrowing on an individual basis. The project experienced a 100 percent repayment rate. When women want larger loans for business enterprises, they are screened by local community leaders and then trained in management, accounting, production, marketing, and quality control (Reno 1981).

Second, intermediary organizations that serve as liaisons between banks and rural women can be set up. These have been very effective in several areas. Women's associations, cooperatives, and banks can assist women in obtaining and establishing credit. The organizations can secure large loans, which they can then lend in smaller amounts to individuals or to locally organized women's groups. They can provide assistance in dealing with banks and government bureaucracies and can incorporate characteristics of the informal financial system preferred by women into their loan programs. Intermediary organizations, in addition to encouraging and helping female borrowers, can also educate the formal financial world about the women's credit needs and the minimal credit risk women represent (Lycette 1984). Two well-known examples of intermediary organizations bridging the gap between women and the banks are SEWA (the Self-Employed Women's Association) and the Working Women's Forum, both of India. These associations organize women into small neighborhood loan groups that grant loans on verbal guarantees in small amounts. They have experienced extremely high repayment rates. Whether or not these loan groups need to be women-only can be determined on a case-by-case basis (Chant 1989; Everett and Savara 1993; Jhabvala 1994).

Third, ensuring women access to agricultural cooperatives is an important goal of any credit project. Information about credit opportunities should be disseminated through channels used by women because large banks, agricultural cooperatives, and extension services have often failed in this regard. Other avenues—such as women's meetings, religious organizations, and the marketplace—can also be effective (Lycette 1984).

The Grameen Bank in Bangladesh is one of the best-known and most successful banking programs in the Third World. It was started in 1976 and has grown into an important source of credit to land-poor rural women, who have been its targeted participants since 1983 and who make up 89 percent of the bank's members. The women form groups of five who share common goals and socioeconomic status. Funds are loaned to individuals or to the group, weekly savings deposits are required of each member, and loans are extended for one year and paid back in small weekly installments. Women have used loans from the Grameen Bank mostly for livestock and poultry raising (50 percent of the loans), processing and manufacturing activities (31 percent), and trading and shopkeeping (19 percent). The bank enjoys a repayment rate of 98 percent of all loans (World Bank 1990).

An example of a small-scale loan project that recognized the need to target women is the Small Farmer Production Project of the Village Bank of the Principal Bank for Development and Agricultural Credit, founded by the Ministry of Agriculture in Egypt. The project was designed to provide loans and extension services to small farmers who own or rent less than five acres of land. In Egypt, 48 percent of women participate in agriculture, and women own 80 percent of household enterprises and 92 percent of dairy enterprises. Because it incorporated features of informal systems of credit, the project met with popularity and success. Local bank managers were given the authority to approve and process loans, reducing the turnaround time from six to eight weeks to two days, thus reducing travel time. In addition, assistance in completing the necessary forms was available, loan terms were flexible, and no collateral was required. Finally, the quality of extension and credit staff was improved through human relations training. The project's specific focus on women's needs and concerns was instrumental in increasing their participation from 8 percent of borrowers in 1983 to over 15 percent in 1985. Women outside the project indicated they would be more likely to participate if more women extension agents were available (Howard-Merriam 1986).

Building on the experiences of the Small Farmer Production Project, the Rural Small Scale Enterprise Project provides credit to female and male entrepreneurs through the Egypt National Bank for Development. Other innovative credit programs have also been developed using formal banking mechanisms (Weidemann 1991).

Projects designed to improve women's access to credit must take into account the characteristics of their targets. Women's legal status regarding inheritance, land ownership, and membership in cooperatives must be clearly understood. Country-specific banking practices that affect women's access to formal credit, such as collateral requirements, must be determined (Arias 1989; Reno 1981). Preliminary studies to determine appropriate loan sizes, interest rates, repayment schedules, and collateral requirements for women should be completed (Buvinic, Sebstad, and Zeidenstein 1979). Of greatest importance is the development of the kinds of credit programs women need and want. Encouraging women to take out loans they do not need and under terms they cannot meet or that will cause dependency or undue hardship is obviously undesirable and inappropriate. Successful formal and informal credit operations in the country and in local areas should be studied to determine what features are most effective and appropriate for women's economic needs and situations. Training, extension services, technical advice, and, where appropriate, analyses of marketing opportunities and realistic prospects for expansion should also be included in the design of credit programs if they are to be successful.

6

APPROPRIATE TECHNOLOGY

Judith Warner and Helen Kreider Henderson

What is appropriate technology? Bryceson (1985:8–9, cited in Stamp 1990: 512) defines technology as those "objects, techniques, skills and processes which facilitate human activity in terms of: first, reducing human energy expenditure, second, reducing labour time, third, improving spatial mobility and fourth, alleviating material uncertainty.... [These] objects, techniques and processes ... have arisen from the application of human understanding and knowledge of matter and ... serve to enhance human capabilities. 'Human capabilities' denote not only an individual's physical and mental capacities but also the social freedom for pursuing one's capacities." This definition suggests that technology is more than a set of skills and materials; it also implies a mode of organizing work (Bourque and Warren 1990; Chaney and Schmink 1976). As Sen (1990:128) notes, "Technology is not only about equipment and its operational characteristics but also about social arrangements that permit the equipment to be used and the so-called productive processes to be carried on."

Appropriate technology for Third World countries is technology that is low in capital costs per unit of output, is highly adaptable to a particular sociocultural environment, is controlled and maintained by those who use it, uses local resources to the greatest extent possible but uses all resources sparingly, and is flexible and adaptable to changing circumstances (see Carr 1985:8–9). Oblepias-Ramos (1991:165) emphasizes that technologies become appropriate "when they carry a deliberate bias for a specific underprivileged sector of a community, as well as an appreciation of that sector's overall physical and cultural environment." Darrow and Pam view appropriate technologies as based on the assumption "that people can and will work together to collectively bring improvements to their communities, recognizing that in most of the world important decisions are made by groups rather than by individuals" (Darrow and Pam 1978, cited in Carr 1985:8).

Technology has different impacts on the lives and work of women and men (Anderson 1985). New technologies have often been introduced to men in subsistence economies without regard for women's and men's traditional roles and with a disruptive impact on people's lives (Nash 1988). Such male-controlled technologies have two common characteristics: (1) they tend to be associated with large-scale commercial production systems designed to produce an economic surplus, and (2) they are controlled by male-dominated bureaucracies (Boulding 1981). Government programs have provided technological inputs and training primarily to men growing cash crops for export rather than to women, who often remain in the subsistence farming sector (Boserup 1970; Carney and Watts 1991; Tinker 1981). Women generally lack access to the training and economic resources that would enable them to acquire new technologies (Stamp 1990; Tinker 1981). Chakravarthy (1992:231) stresses that "the impact of the new technologies needs to be assessed in a total context," which includes "equitable distribution of assets, wages and productivity, skill formation and training, and institutional and organizational support particularly with credit and marketing."

Governments and development agencies continue to view technology as gender neutral and value free—an inaccurate perception, as can be seen from the examples of failed projects cited in this chapter and elsewhere in this volume (see also Bindocci 1993). Agarwal (1992a:261) points out that examples of participative projects for technology transfer from the ground up that incorporate gender issues serve as reminders not only of what is possible but also of "the need for more comprehensive social changes if these experiments are to become general and wide-based." As Bagchi (1993:156) notes, new technologies have sometimes deprived women of employment but at other times have brought them new opportunities for employment and escape from labor-intensive daily toil. Development projects that introduce technology and which consider women as a target group outside their social, cultural, and geographic context, or which fail to consider women's multiple roles within that context, risk worsening women's conditions rather than improving their quality of life.

Development planners must closely examine the concept of appropriate technology to ensure that gender issues are taken into account. Who decides what is appropriate? Whose interests are served by the new technologies? Who makes the decisions about what kinds of technologies are to be introduced? In the past, these and related questions have not been posed, and the assumption that technology is gender neutral and value free has guided its transfer and introduction, often to the detriment of women (Chakravarthy 1992).

TECHNOLOGY AND THE GENDER DIVISION OF LABOR

When women are included in development planning, they are often seen as passive recipients of development aid rather than productive members of society (Stamp 1990). This attitude excludes women and their productive labor from participation in development and results in their marginalization within society. In some areas, traditional gender divisions of labor have begun to change as women have become involved in development. For instance, Ogana (1989) describes a community water project in Kenya in which women work closely with unrelated men and attend training classes with men—both of which are significant breaks with tradition and are gaining women greater participation in community decision making and access to technology.

Household task linkages are an important consideration in development planning, especially those linkages involving gender-differentiated or gender-sequential activities, such as food processing (Ahmed 1985). If new technologies require an increased labor contribution from men or offer them the opportunity to earn more money, women's work will increase in areas from which men withdraw. This has often been the case where cash cropping is intensified and women remain in or are relegated to subsistence cropping. Women's productivity, however, may be increased by new technologies that are dependent on male output. Ahmed (1985) notes that the introduction of hand-operated oil presses can increase women's ability to process palm oil but that women's oil production is undercut unless men supply sufficient quantities of palm fruits. In contrast, the introduction to Ghanian women of a new cassava grater for gari making was successful because men concurrently increased production of cassava to take advantage of the expanded capacity created by the grater (Date-Bah 1985).

Rural women perform many household maintenance activities that are essential to the support of the family. Numerous studies have documented that rural women in many regions of the Third World work longer hours than their male counterparts and have less personal or leisure time (Cain

1981; Chakravarthy 1992; McSweeney 1979a; Oblepias-Ramos 1991; Stamp 1990). Rural women regard time spent in food processing and water and fuel portage as especially onerous. Clearly, technology aimed at easing those burdens would have great social value. The economic value of household-related technologies is not obvious, however, so those technologies associated with commercial production have received much more attention (Stamp 1990; Staudt 1979). Bourque and Warren (1990:88) warn that technology introduced to lighten women's work in the home may create a sexual division of technology wherein women gain access to new techniques for domestic labor while men acquire technologies more applicable to employment and income generation.

Because women often use the time saved on one task to perform some other household task, the introduction of appropriate technologies does not necessarily lessen women's workload. In Burkina Faso, the Equal Access to Education Project introduced donkey carts to help with fuel portage. The reduction of time spent on fuel portage was significant, and that aspect of the project was a phenomenal success. Many of the women used the time they saved for other household activities, such as water portage or cotton spinning—an income-generating activity. The new technology increased the quality and level of activities in which women participated, yet it did not decrease women's time spent on household work. The goal of the project—increased time for women to spend on functional literacy education—was not realized, but the villagers' quality of life and health were favorably affected (McSweeney and Freedman 1980).

The economic importance of labor-saving technologies for women becomes evident when a broader range of consequences is considered. A labor-saving innovation is beneficial if (1) it allows women to spend less time providing basic needs and more time on their preferred productive activities; (2) it meets a need for competitive, low-cost technology using renewable energy when energy costs are high (Staudt 1979); and (3) women's health improves due to a trend toward less strenuous labor requirements, where women's health is viewed as an important factor in shaping the health and development of the family and community.

CHARACTERISTICS OF APPROPRIATE TECHNOLOGY

In recent years, the indigenous knowledge of local people in Third World countries has begun to gain recognition and respect (Dirar 1992; Oblepias-Ramos 1991; Stamp 1990; for a history of changing attitudes toward technology on the part of development planners and scholars, see Bourque and Warren 1990). Dirar (1992), for example, reviews food fermentation technologies invented and practiced by African women. Scientists investigating methods of preserving and improving the nutritional quality of available foods have been impressed with traditional techniques used by the women, which they developed over generations. "With respect to food technology," Dirar emphasized, "the African woman has vast knowledge which must form the basis for development in this area" (1992:23).

The first characteristic of appropriate technology is its reliance on the knowledge, abilities, and needs of local people. Any introduced technologies should be understood and controlled by the people themselves. The following criteria form a basis for assessing the suitability of technology.

Low Cost

Appropriate technology is affordable. Because rural women often have limited incomes, project inputs should be within their economic reach, and the women should have access to credit and a reasonable chance of being able to repay loans (Hoskins, n.d.).

Durability

Appropriate technology is durable and easy to maintain. Too often women have become involved with projects that distribute complicated mechanical equipment that breaks down. Technology transfer has a much greater chance of success if women are trained in the production and maintenance of new and locally based machinery (Hoskins n.d.; Stamp 1990) and if that machinery is built to be long-lasting.

Profitability

Appropriate technologies offer the possibility of increasing women's income. Savings can come in the form of time, labor, or money (Stevens 1985). Profitability is also affected by access to markets. It is of no use to produce a commodity that cannot be sold locally if women cannot obtain low-cost transportation to markets.

Efficiency

Appropriate technologies enable women to increase the quality or quantity of their traditional products (Carr 1984). "Improved" stoves have been introduced in many Third World countries without considering women's time constraints or preferences. For example, solar stoves require adjustment throughout the day, taking time away from other tasks. An open hearth in the house provides warmth and light at night, which may be missing from a more efficient but enclosed stove (Adams and Solomon 1991). These types of considerations determine how "efficient" a new technology may be.

Cultural Compatibility

Introduced technologies should be culturally acceptable and able to fit into women's (or men's) current work patterns (Carr 1984 and 1991; Nash 1988; Stevens 1985). Often the traditional goods and services that women provide can be upgraded by appropriate technologies, and new or modified products can be made more competitive with those produced by capital-intensive industries (Carr 1984). The introduction to Ghanian women of mechanical graters and pressing machines for processing of cassava for gari, noted above, was successful because appropriate characteristics were incorporated (Date-Bah 1985). While increasing women's output, these devices cost little and did not represent a drastic change from previous production techniques. Such experience indicates that the technological innovations that are most likely to be adopted by women are those that fit their needs, constraints, and opportunities.

Oxby (1991:207) notes that many societies are in the midst of significant cultural change and that "attitudes towards women's roles may also be changing. One should also ask who precisely feels these constraints, in order to make an appropriate response: is it all of the community, or is it particular individuals? Could it be some of the project personnel?"

ACCESS TO APPROPRIATE TECHNOLOGY

Women must own and be able to maintain new technologies. Carr (1984) indicates that serious social constraints on women's access to technology include poor organization or poor project management, credit problems, and a lack of time, training, and support from husbands or the community. Control over technology also includes access to and control over the resources women require in order to use and benefit from the technology. According to Oblepias-Ramos (1991:163), these resources include "training in attitudes, knowledge, and skills as well as access to capital, and extension assistance." Recognition of women's roles as decision makers in technology transfer projects is also vital to their access to new technologies (Stamp 1990).

An attempt to deal with these issues is illustrated by the Inter-American Commission of Women, which conducted the Appropriate Technology for Rural Women Project (the Proyecto de Tecnología Apropiada para Mujeres Campesinas, or PTAMC), initiated in Bolivia and Ecuador and later extended to other Latin American countries (Flora 1985). PTAMC was designed to create women's organizations to assist in introducing appropriate technologies for agriculture, animal husbandry, cottage industries, and domestic tasks to rural Andean communities. In forming women's organizations at the community level, PTAMC was careful to link up with existing community groups. Training focused on specific skills that members could draw upon in community development projects. PTAMC stressed motivating community members to generate their own ideas for projects, organize the activities, and contribute their own labor. PTAMC's input was seen as the provision of information, advice, and links to other development resources, marketing assistance, and the donation of capital at critical points in project implementation.

Involving women's organizations encouraged women to offer their own input regarding their needs and targets. PTAMC conducted a survey of women's time use, and after evaluating the survey results, the project offered income enhancement opportunities to women that did not interfere with their other responsibilities. Later, women had the opportunity to develop skills in working with the machinery PTAMC brought in, a chance that was rarely available outside the project. In the most successful organizations, men also became involved with the group. This increased community cohesiveness because the organization was viewed as "working for the community through women, rather than just for women" (Flora 1985:16).

The degree of project success varied widely among the communities involved. A key to success was ensuring that the technology remained appropriate and maintainable through the resources of both material and time available to the community. The most successful income-generation projects used locally available materials and satisfied local community needs for services and goods rather than relying on undependable external markets.

INCOME GENERATION

Rural women themselves are the best decision makers regarding income-generating projects involving new technologies. Income-generating projects introduced by outsiders often assume that women's most basic need is income, whereas rural women working as agricultural producers have many other basic needs as well, including clean water, fuel, food, and health care (Stamp 1990).

Income-generating projects that fail to consider women may increase output but at the same time decrease women's employment or involvement in the production process. Rice hullers and oil presses, introduced without considering who will control the new machinery, may remove women from processes they formerly performed by hand and from which they were able to earn an income. For instance, Chakravarthy (1992:229) cites a project in India in which machines were introduced to prepare tobacco for rolling, traditionally women's work. As a result, 96 percent of women's waged work in the study area was lost.

Examples of successful income-generating projects using appropriate technology to provide rural goods and services do exist (see, e.g., Adams and Solomon 1991; *Appropriate Technology* 1991; Carr 1978, 1984, 1985; Rai 1989; Sandhu and Sandler 1986; Stamp 1990). One illustrative example is a fruit and vegetable preserving project in Honduras. A women's club initiated a vegetable and fruit bottling business with the help of a UNICEF loan. Prior to the project, women were unfamiliar with the food preservation techniques, but project training and investment in kitchen equipment (pots, bottles, lids, and knives, for example) enabled the women to get started. At last report, the women were repaying the loan with one-third of their profits, and local families had doubled their income (Carr 1984). In 1991 the journal *Appropriate Technology* reported on a project designed to produce and market improved pottery stoves in Kenya. Most of the women potters had previously made decorative items for sale. Some are now working nearly full-time producing the Maendeleo, an efficient wood-burning stove that is growing in popularity. The stove serves multiple functions: it provides women potters with a source of income, it reduces the amount of firewood needed by women to cook household meals, and its introduction and manufacture have been a catalyst for organizing women's groups.

CAPITAL-INTENSIVE VERSUS LABOR-INTENSIVE TECHNOLOGY

Capital-intensive technology often has had the effect of easing women out of the formal economic sector, whereas technologies that focus on local needs, labor supply, resources, and value are generally more appropriate to the economic and survival needs of rural women. In Third World nations the appropriate technologies may be labor-intensive, may require little capital and little maintenance, and may not demand high levels of Western-style education. Further, the materials they require are more easily purchased and used by low-income people, especially women, than more expensive "high" technologies (Adams and Solomon 1991).

Stamp (1990) describes a capital-intensive bakery project in Zambia, where modern bakeries had been built in towns without considering the impact on women, who had previously baked most of the local bread. She also describes, in contrast, the introduction of capital-intensive technology—corn mills—that benefited women in Cameroon. Women have been running and profiting from the mills since the 1950s. As Stamp (1990:53) concludes, "It is only when, by coincidence or design, women collectively appropriate capital-intensive technology . . . that such success stories can be told. In other words, the miracle of technology lies not in its physical attributes but in its enlightened application."

With any type of technology, development planners must ask who will introduce it, who will own it, who will control it, who will maintain it, and who will benefit from it. When planners fail to address these questions, negative consequences often result for sizable numbers of the population, and too often many of those affected are women. In Indonesia, for example, government schemes to increase rice production introduced high-yield seed varieties and mechanized production. Traditional methods of harvesting and distributing rice were locally based and labor-intensive. Most of the harvesters were women, who used small finger knives to harvest the rice and who received a portion of the harvest as their pay. Hulling was done by hand and again paid in kind. With the introduction of high-yield varieties and mechanized rice hullers, harvesting is done by men with sickles, and men own and operate the hullers. While the mechanical rice hullers are much faster and more economically efficient than hand pounding, women who were formerly employed as hullers have been displaced by male owned and operated hullers and have lost an important source of rice to feed themselves and their families. Cultural and economic factors restricted women's access to the new technologies, which have met the goal of increased rice production but have exacerbated rather than alleviating rural unemployment. Unfortunately, government planning did not include the development of alternative employment for the displaced women (Cain 1981; Nash 1988).

Appropriate cropping technology and agricultural intensification can prove advantageous for rural women (Bagchi 1993). In Asia, women have traditionally worked as household and wage laborers in such labor-intensive rice production activities as transplanting, weeding, and harvesting.

Unnevehr (1985) suggests that women would benefit from the introduction of labor-intensive, short-statured, fertilizer-responsive modern rice. Such rice also requires increased irrigation and cropping intensification, which would create a stable demand for women agricultural laborers throughout the year.

Women have traditionally been involved in productive processes requiring skill and organization, but the introduction of new technologies in Third World countries has too often been implemented without regard for women's needs and abilities. Writing of the group Approtech Asia, Oblepias-Ramos (1991:164) states that the organization "is founded on the very firm belief that it cannot be morally tenable for the other half of humanity to have to struggle to deal with basic existence." As Bourque and Warren (1990:100) succinctly state, "one realizes how much technology and education are bearers of social relations marked by gender. Access [to technology] is not enough to change these gendered asymmetries, though it is clearly crucial to the process of change in the forms of education and in the uses of technology." Carr (1991:13) further strengthens this argument when she adds: "Providing small farmers, and women in particular, with information on existing technologies does not result in technology transfer if the technology is not appropriate to their needs or if they do not have the necessary skills to interpret it and put it to use. The introduction of improved technologies to women therefore involves the transfer not only of information, but also of skills in ways that encourage the development and utilization of indigenous resources." Clearly, a wide range of gender issues must be taken into account when contemplating the introduction of new technologies.

7

AGRICULTURAL EXTENSION

Catherine Besteman

Agricultural extension and training services are major mechanisms by which new technologies and information are introduced in development and assistance programs. Special attention to gender issues is crucial in this area because of the major contributions women make to the agricultural economy (Blumberg 1992). In some areas, such as Africa, wives and husbands may farm separate fields and keep separate accounts. Where this is the case and where the gender division of labor in agriculture is strong, delivering extension services and disseminating technological information to women are especially critical. Extension services do not regularly reach women farmers, however (Walker 1990). According to Saito and Weidemann, this bias toward male farmers is "sometimes by design, but more often by default" (1990:i). It results from traditional perspectives and attitudes on the part of male extension agents, development planners, and farmers (Saito and Spurling 1992).

Throughout the world, male farmers are the primary recipients of training in the new technologies and mechanization that allow them to move into cash cropping and that increasingly give female farmers the sole responsibility for subsistence crops or force them out of agriculture entirely (Anderson 1984; Dauber and Cain 1981). Shiferraw (1985) notes that women's development projects in rural Africa offered no appropriate training for women displaced from the agricultural economy following the introduction of mechanization. Because men are given more opportunities, the existing gap between male farmers and female farmers, who tend to be poorer, is widened. Agricultural development projects present ideal opportunities to narrow this gap and to expose all farmers to newer technologies and agricultural techniques.

It can be argued, based on economies of scale, that increasing the production of large farms and consolidating small farms result in more efficient agricultural production. However, the goal of efficiency of production must be considered in the context of the intended beneficiaries and weighed against issues of equity. Forcing large numbers of small-scale farmers off the land is generally unjust, as well as extremely costly, inefficient, and unproductive in economies that lack the ability to absorb these people in other sectors. Raising production on all farms, large and small, is more efficient in the long run (for more information, see Chambers and Ghildyal 1985; Netting 1993; Silliman and Lenton 1985; and Tinker 1990).

THE DISSEMINATION OF INFORMATION TO FARMERS

Many development projects have attempted to introduce change based on the assumption that if men receive training and extension assistance, they will pass this information along to female farmers in the area. Recent studies have shown this assumption to be faulty (Carloni and Horenstein 1986; Due 1988; Potash 1985; Saito and Spurling 1992; Saito and Weidemann 1990; Spring 1988; Staudt 1985). Organizations involved in extension work reported that, for all of Africa in 1988 and 1989, 7 percent of services were devoted to women (Blumberg 1992). Extension agents frequently establish and maintain contacts with only a small number of male farmers. These "contact farmers" do not necessarily or even usually share information with female farmers (Saito and Spurling 1992; Saito and Weidemann 1990). In some areas, contact farmers must be literate in order to participate in extension programs. This further limits women's access to extension services because, as noted earlier, more women than men are illiterate, especially in rural areas (Saito and Weidemann 1990).

Staudt's (1985) study in western Kenya found that women provided the majority of the agricultural labor and managed two-fifths of the farms, yet the political and administrative networks through which information was passed and contracts were made were dominated by men, and women-managed farms received fewer services at all levels than jointly managed farms. These gaps increased with the value of the services, from small differentials in demonstration plots and home visits to huge differentials in specialized training and credit programs. Staudt found these differences to exist in areas with intensive service delivery, between poor male and female farmers, and between wealthier male and female farmers. In other words, service delivery and specialized training favored male farmers in all study areas and at all socioeconomic levels.

Staudt attributes this discrepancy to several factors. First, prejudicial attitudes toward women farmers on the part of extension workers reflect male extension workers' predisposition to see women farmers in limited roles. Second, women's invisibility means that women are excluded from opportunities to obtain extension services. Announcements about group demonstrations were made at *barazas* (community meetings attended mostly by men). Specialized training courses offered for one- to two-week periods were attended primarily by men because information regarding openings at the training center was passed through male networks. Female farmers who do the majority of farming, even if invited, would often have logistical problems in attending due to their daily household responsibilities. Third, women comprise only 2 percent of the field staff in Kenya's agricultural extension service. To change the pre-existing policies of recruitment and service delivery would have required energy and commitment that may not have been present within the ministry responsible for extension services.

Saito and Weidemann (1990:4–5) add more limiting factors to this list: (1) the perception on the part of extension agents that women have little decision-making authority on the farm; (2) women's heavy workload, which limits the time they have to meet with extension agents; (3) extensionists' and women's social and religious views, which may inhibit their working together; (4) the possibility that extension agents view women as physically unable to farm; and (5) the perception that women will not understand most extension information. In addition, where women are viewed solely as subsistence farmers, extension agents may conclude that women do not need their services or information (Mencher 1993).

Male extension workers in Zambia organized a workshop to demonstrate to men and women farmers a field-measuring technique. The male farmers sat around the male extension agent in the shade of a tree while the women sat a short distance away in the cooking area of the compound where the workshop took place. The women were unable to hear the presentation, and when the men went to a nearby field to see the demonstration, the women all went home (Carr 1991:31). These examples highlight the fact that unless women are specifically targeted by extension agents, they are easily left out of proceedings because of cultural or institutional factors.

In areas where women do the majority of agricultural work, extension agents who do not interact with women can be a great hindrance to the success of development efforts (Due 1988). In a project in Zambia, data indicate that more women than men were low-resource farmers and that in these poorer environments, local varieties of agricultural produce—most often grown by women—were more productive than improved varieties (Hildebrand and Poey 1985). By ignoring women and the constraints on them, extension workers may be leaving out those who perform the majority of farm work and who could most benefit from training and access to resources.

RECRUITING EXTENSIONISTS

The lack of trained female agricultural extension agents has been noted throughout the world. In the Third World, women make up a small proportion of the agricultural extension staff. This figure varies by region as follows: Africa, 3 percent; Latin America and the Caribbean, 14 percent; Asia and Oceania, 23 percent (Spring 1988:409). To compound matters, a large proportion of female agricultural extension workers are actually employed in home economics, not in agriculture (Berger, Delancey, and Mellencamp 1984; Blumberg 1992; Spring 1988).

To deal effectively with women's farming needs, more female extension agents need to be recruited, and those who are recruited need to be given better training in agriculture instead of weaving, cloth dyeing, soap making, and basketry, the training most frequently offered by African rural development projects for women (Shiferraw 1985). Saito and Spurling (1992) note that home economists constitute an undervalued and underutilized resource in many countries, and they could be retrained to provide much-needed agricultural extension services.

Other issues are involved in the recruitment and deployment of women as agricultural extensionists. In Nepal, for example, because women's literacy rates are lower than men's, fewer women qualify for entrance into training programs (Davenport, Nickell, and Pradhan 1986). In Zambia, very few of the small number of women extension agents go through the two-year training program required to obtain a certificate and become an agricultural assistant. Instead, women agents remain concentrated in home economics programs. Women at higher levels in Zambia's extension program are mainly located in central offices in more urbanized provinces rather than in field offices in rural provinces, where more women farmers and women-headed households are found (Carr 1991:29–30). In Botswana, one major reason for the small number of female graduates from the agricultural college is simply the lack of facilities for female students (Carr 1991:49).

In many areas of the world, women's families may discourage them from seeking training and employment as extensionists for fear they will be assigned to largely male teams in rural areas, thus endangering their reputation and chance for marriage. Clearly, special attention must be paid to cultural constraints and concerns in the recruitment and training of both male and female extension workers in agricultural schools (Brush 1986; Saito and Weidemann 1990). Even after they are trained, however, institutional barriers deter women from advancing as professionals in agriculture. In Côte d'Ivoire, for example, the social and educational systems are structured in such a way that women are discouraged at every level from continuing into higher education. As girls they are more likely to be kept on the farm to provide labor while boys receive education and training, and as adults women are valued most highly if they are married and have children. As competition for the limited number of places in agricultural colleges and the small number of jobs increases, women are further disadvantaged. Men tend to be better prepared for the college entrance examinations; women are outnumbered by men in all higher levels of education; and admission policies of the agriculture colleges have favored men over women (Brunet-Perrault and Doss 1992).

TRAINING EXTENSIONISTS

Simply increasing the number of female extension agents will not solve the problem of how to disseminate more information to female farmers. First, both male and female extensionists need to be trained in issues relating to gender, such as the importance of targeting female as well as male farmers. In one Kenyan project, although 15 percent of the agricultural extension workers are women, all of the farmers contacted by the project were men (Carloni and Horenstein 1986).

Second, extensionists must learn to collect household information about who does the farming in the household, how the agricultural work is organized, what crops are grown and how they are used, and what resources are available to individual members of the household (Potash 1985; Spring 1988). In one case—the Integrated Cereals Project in Nepal, funded by USAID—female farmers reported doing 79 percent of all agricultural work and 35 percent of all decision making. While female extension agents agreed with these figures, male extensionists said women did only some of the work and no decision making (Shrestha et al. 1984).

Third, extensionists need to be aware of how best to deliver their information. They must discover what information is disseminated through which channels (kin, male or female networks, mass media, community meetings, etc.) so that they can more effectively make information available to women (Dixon-Mueller 1985). Then, if training courses seem the best solution, they should be held in villages so that women who cannot leave their domestic responsibilities to attend courses offered outside the area will have the opportunity to participate. Trained and paid local paraprofessionals comprise another option for more efficiently disseminating information (Staudt 1985).

Age barriers face both women and men extensionists. In many traditional societies, young people are not expected or allowed to give advice to older people, and newly graduated extensionists may have a difficult time bringing new ideas to older male or female farmers (Brunet-Perrault and Doss 1992). Thus training in assertiveness and sensitivity in dealing with contact farmers is a necessary part of the education of extensionists.

EXAMPLES OF SUCCESS

Some projects have successfully integrated gender issues into their extension and training components. As a result of its Women in Agriculture Development Project, the Ministry of Agriculture of Malawi issued a circular to extension agents advising them to target female smallholders. The circular provides suggestions and methods for how male extensionists can contact and work with female farmers (Spring 1988).

Training for male extension agents can improve their knowledge of women farmers' needs and their ability to communicate with them. Extension materials developed especially for women, and training in their use, can make male extensionists' contacts with female farmers more successful. Some programs use a female extension agent to make the initial contact with women farmers or women's groups. Once they establish communication and gain people's trust, the contact farmers are then introduced to the regular extension agent for their area, usually a male, and the female agent moves on to the next group. This gender-targeting technique is one of the successful innovations introduced in northwestern Cameroon by the government's Development Mission (Walker 1990).

A project in Jamaica successfully added a women's component to an existing agricultural project. The component, developed as an integral part of the overall project, recruited and trained young women as home extension officers and started a home gardening project (Chaney 1981). Extension workers in Ecuador recruited a bilingual Quechua and Spanish speaker when it became apparent that the language barrier was prohibiting them from working with women farmers. A female Quechua speaker worked as a translator for the Spanish-speaking extension agents. Because of her traditional dress and her knowledge of Quechua, she was able to establish a rapport with the Quechua women that had been lacking with the Spanish-speaking extension agents (Garrett and Espinosa 1994).

The Arid and Semi-Arid Lands Project in Kenya, administered by the government of Kenya and USAID, provides a final example (Carloni and Horenstein 1986). Although 60 percent of the farms in the project area were operated by women, almost all the farmers contacted through the original training and visitation system were men. Midway through the project, operators discovered that the innovations introduced by the extensionists to the contact farmers were not spreading to other farmers. As the authors point out, "The weakest link in the system [of extension service delivery] is the relationship between the contact farmer and the other members of the extension group" (Carloni and Horenstein 1986:341). As a result of this discovery, the project was redesigned to target local community mutual assistance groups (*mwethya* groups) for meetings and information dispersal. Women comprise 90 percent of the elected officials of these groups. This project provides a good example of how shortcomings in design can be modified and adapted in midcourse to meet the needs of the people a project is intended to serve. Other examples of successful efforts to change the ways extension services are offered to farmers in Third World countries are described in Feldstein and Jiggins 1994, Blumberg 1992, Feldstein and Poats 1989, Saito and Spurling 1992, and Saito and Weidemann 1990.

In sum, the three primary areas of concern regarding gender issues in agricultural extension and training are (1) the recruitment of extensionists, especially women; (2) the training of extensionists, both male and female; and (3) the dissemination of information to farmers, particularly female farmers. Much work remains to be done to ensure that women farmers receive adequate extension services and that women are encouraged to become extension agents (Singamma Sreenivasan Foundation 1993). Until the extent and importance of women's contributions to agricultural production are perceived and this perception is built into extension programs as a matter of course, women farmers will continue to need special consideration. The examples noted in this chapter make it clear that improvements in extension services can be made if women farmers are specifically targeted.

8

OUT-MIGRATION

Catherine Besteman

The impact of out-migration on rural production systems is of growing concern to development planners. In 1980 there were between 20 and 21 million migrant workers worldwide (Bohning 1984, cited in Palmer 1985), and today 100 million people are living as legal or illegal immigrants (ILO 1994). In many areas of the world, men comprise the majority of migrants, moving primarily to urban and industrial areas and leaving women behind to maintain life in the rural areas (Boserup 1970; Chaney 1980; Momsen and Townsend 1987; UN 1991). Africa, especially southern Africa, exhibits the widest gap in the sex ratio of male to female migrants. From 40 to 60 percent of all married women in Lesotho have emigrant husbands, and in Botswana, 43 percent of rural households are headed by women, indicating high levels of male out-migration (Palmer 1985). Recent censuses, however, show that African women are also migrating to cities in increasing numbers, searching for employment, especially when men migrate to obtain work and women are not able to sustain the household through commercial or subsistence agriculture (Adepoju 1994:31).

In Latin America, women have dominated the migratory flow during the past 20 years (Chaney 1980; UN 1991). In some Latin American countries, girls under 15 make up the majority of internal migrants (UN 1991). The forces pushing and pulling women from rural areas in Latin America and the Caribbean are highly complex and must be analyzed in a site-specific manner (CAM 1987; Chant 1992; Momsen 1992; Monk 1993; Monk and Alexander 1986; Radcliffe 1992; Young 1982). Further, the effects of both female and male out-migration on local agricultural production must be examined in all areas of the Third World.

EFFECTS OF MALE OUT-MIGRATION

Out-migration is of concern to development planners because population shifts and changing sex ratios in sending and receiving areas affect project design and implementation. Because women often are left as the primary farmers when men migrate, successful projects will need to be designed with the specific needs of these female farmers and household heads in mind.

Labor Concerns

Rural women whose husbands have migrated face a number of problems. As they often assume the primary responsibility for farm production in addition to household management, their work increases, sometimes dramatically. Thus the gender division of labor in a project area should be of prime concern to planners, especially where women farmers experience difficulty in accomplishing male tasks. The deficit of male family labor resulting from the husband's absence is frequently not alleviated by contributions from other male members of a woman's extended family, as is often assumed (Palmer 1985). The cost of hiring male labor to replace absent household members is often prohibitive, particularly to women-headed households (Adepoju 1994), and women may find it difficult to penetrate and participate in male labor networks. Male tasks, such as plowing, may be left undone or performed less frequently or later in households without resident males than in those with them (Palmer 1985; Peters 1986; Whitehead 1994; see also Chap. 9). When male labor is available for hire, cultural attitudes toward gender relationships in areas of authority and the division of labor may cause problems for women who need to hire and supervise male workers (Carr 1991).

Studies of the Third World suggest that agricultural production drops as a result of male out-migration and the resulting scarcity of male labor (Arizpe and Botey 1987; Chant 1992; ICRW 1979). This may be true even as women's labor increases to compensate for absent males, as women themselves may migrate to perform paid agricultural or other labor (Chant 1992; Shobha 1987). In some regions of Latin America, women become more involved in subsistence agriculture as men migrate (Nash and Safa 1986). Ferrán and Pessar (1991), writing of the Dominican Republic, trace a cycle of change in agriculture: first, land is consolidated into the hands of fewer owners as the successful farmers buy the land of the less successful;

later, the land is subdivided among the heirs of the successful farmers, eventually creating plots too small for even subsistence production. These factors result in increasing landlessness and out-migration (in the case of the Dominican Republic, often to the United States), a decreasing availability of agricultural labor, and a growing percentage of income spent on food because it is no longer produced by the household.

Women often cultivate less land when they have the primary responsibility for farm production and are sometimes compelled to abandon land. They also practice more extensive forms of agriculture as a result of their greater workload. In areas of Botswana where land is allocated to households by local chiefs, female-headed households farm 35 percent less land than male-headed households. This is due primarily to labor and draft animal shortages experienced by female-headed households (Horn and Nkambule-Kanyima 1984). Due (1991) cites studies from Zambia and Tanzania showing that female-headed households planted less acreage, devoted a higher proportion of their land to subsistence food crops, had a much lower total value of crop production, received fewer visits from extension agents, and relied more heavily on diverse income-generating activities than households where both a man and a woman were present.

Financial Concerns

In addition to the effects of decreased availability of male labor, women in women-headed households take on greater decision-making responsibilities, some of which are related to household finances. Some women whose husbands have migrated receive remittances, but others do not, or they receive small or irregular payments and so must find other means of generating income to support their families. Women who receive remittances may not have the authority to make decisions regarding the use of the money in farming activities. They may instead have to wait until their husbands return, or they may have to consult with male members of their extended family. The question of remittances is of vital interest to development planners, who should inquire about who receives remittances, how much is sent, who has the authority over expenditures, and what is purchased.

In some cases, a migrant husband may earmark remittance money for certain purposes. If remittances are not intended for agricultural investment, it may be because migration was a result of limited opportunities for agricultural investment. In Lesotho, for example, where men migrate to South Africa to work in the mines, most women do not receive remittances from migrant husbands (UN 1991). A farming wife is expected by her migrant husband to meet household consumption needs with her own cash and subsistence cultivation. A lack of male family labor or money to hire labor results in a drop in agricultural production in women-headed households. To meet household needs, women often depend on nonfarm means of raising income, such as brewing and selling beer (Bisilliat and Fieloux 1987; Palmer 1985). Women in the Dominican Republic most often continue to depend on their migrant husbands as major income earners and decision makers. Decisions about planting crops and pastures and buying livestock, for example, are made during the husband's visits home, by letter, or through visiting relatives (Georges 1990).

The Middle East presents a varied picture. In Egypt, mothers encourage their unmarried sons to migrate and send remittances in order to pay bridewealth, whereas wives encourage their husbands to migrate in order to provide funds to set up a separate household from the parents-in-law. Mothers or wives allocate remittance money used to purchase food (Brink 1991). Remittance money applied toward consumption often results in increased purchases of imported foods. In other areas, migrant husbands send their remittances to male family members who have been appointed guardians of the wife in the husband's absence. Pakistani men send remittances to their fathers rather than to their wives and earmark the money for debt repayment or land purchases (UN 1991). Similarly, in Bangladesh, migrants usually send remittance money to other males of the household or to women of greater status than the wife. Women with migrant husbands may gain status, but their authority within the household does not seem to change (Islam and Perveen 1984). Connell's research in the South Pacific showed that women's status may actually decline if their husbands migrate and leave them behind in strained economic circumstances (Connell 1984).

New Opportunities for Women

Linked to the use of remittance money is women's opportunity to participate in cooperatives and to receive credit and training in agricultural techniques. In situations in which women receive remittances and exercise some control over their use, their investment opportunities continue to be limited if they are excluded from training courses or barred from receiving credit (see Chap. 6).

Rural areas with high rates of male out-migration are experiencing declining levels of labor availability, land productivity, and cultivated land. Where women have not been included in training in the use of modern agricultural technology, the use of such technology is also declining as men leave (ICRW 1979; Stamp 1990). The causes and effects of male out-migration are critical aspects of development planning in many areas. Factors related to out-migration—the changing gender division of labor, the effects of a declining supply of male labor on female farmers, the use of remittances, participation in decision making, and women farmers' access to technology, training, and credit—are all essential issues in community planning.

Palmer (1985) suggests a number of points for consideration by planners designing rural projects in areas of male out-migration. Because migration may be caused by a lack of local agricultural opportunities, investment to upgrade the local environment may create realistic opportunities for agricultural investment. Migrants' wives require access to services—including new technologies, training, extension, credit, and cooperatives—for both marketing and agriculture. If the husband determines the use of remittances, extension agents can meet with both the husband and wife during the husband's home visits. This might provide the male migrant with more insights into what happens on the farm during his absence and may encourage him to earmark remittance money for agricultural purposes. Knowledge of women's on-farm and off-farm division of labor is essential to understanding their strategies and critical to planners' abilities to design projects that address women's needs. Improving the profitability of women's activities helps them meet their cash needs, and programs for rotating credit funds can be designed to help women farmers through times when remittances are not available and cash is in short supply. Such programs may help to dissuade these women from partially or completely abandoning farmland. Subsidizing tractor services or training women to fill the labor gaps left by male out-migration could decrease the workload of migrants' wives and help them maintain levels of farm output. Labor-saving appropriate technology may help reduce the demands on women's time and increase labor efficiency, especially in the domestic arena. Whitehead (1994) stresses that not all women who remain in agricultural areas when men migrate become poverty-stricken. Some women have benefited from increased involvement in commercial production or substantial remittances.

WOMEN MIGRANTS

Women are leaving rural areas in increasing numbers in many areas of the Third World. In Latin America, women dominate rural-to-urban internal migration (Crummett 1985, 1987). Male and female migration in Latin America and the Caribbean is linked to the decline of smallholder agriculture and the indebtedness of small-scale farmers (Chaney 1980, 1983). Young (1982) showed that education in rural areas tended to create a relative surplus of young women, who then migrated to cities in search of jobs not available in the countryside. The "pull" factors of urban areas—such as perceived opportunities for a better job and higher urban wages—draw women from the countryside. In Botswana, women form the bulk of the rural-to-urban migration stream because they cannot meet their needs in agricultural production. This is primarily due to male out-migration, especially in cases in which women receive no remittances (Horn and Nkambule-Kanyima 1984).

In an interesting variation, some women in the Dominican Republic whose husbands migrated to find work in the United States returned to rural areas from the cities where they had previously lived. In part this was because it was less expensive for the women to live with their families in the country than to stay in the city, but it was also because they wanted to avoid gossip about their behavior that might reach their migrant husbands (Georges 1990). Chant (1992) discusses rural-to-urban migration in Costa Rica, where families have moved as units to small towns in the mostly rural northwest of the country. Many women become permanent town dwellers, dependent on the seasonal migration of male household members, who follow agricultural employment opportunities in the surrounding countryside. Others occasionally migrate themselves in order to participate in seasonal wage labor, harvesting coffee or working as domestic servants.

The experiences of returning female migrants must also be considered. These women represent a skilled or potentially skilled labor force. Providing opportunities for them to utilize their productive abilities should be one focus of rural agricultural projects. Returning migrants often are agents of change and can play an active role in community organizing. Klaufert (n.d.), for example, describes how a group of returning female migrants in a Burkina Faso village organized to establish a local clinic. Projects in rural areas can be designed to address the factors driving the out-migration of men and women. Vocational training, agricultural training, education, and credit should be some of the target issues for projects designed to meet the needs of women farmers.

FORCED MIGRATION, RESETTLEMENT, AND REFUGEES

In at least the past twenty years, international attention has focused on mass movements of people in response to political unrest, environmental disasters, poverty, and other causes. Estimates place the total number of refugees worldwide at 20 million, with another 20 million people displaced within their own countries (Martin 1991; Taft 1987). Women comprise 80 percent of all refugees and displaced persons (UN 1991). The issue of resettlement is addressed in Chapter 11. Voluntary resettlement in the form of government-sponsored or spontaneous colonization schemes in frontier areas is quite distinct from the population movement involved in forced migration and the flight of refugees. An expanding literature illuminates the growing awareness of the problems faced by women, children, and men whose lives have been uprooted and forever changed (see Martin 1991; UNHCR 1989).

Refugee movements pose serious problems in many Third World countries. Movements of displaced people have often been from one rural area of a Third World country to another, which places strains on the infrastructure and resources of countries that may not be successfully dealing with their own internal problems. In Ethiopia, political unrest and war heightened local problems of soil depletion and deforestation. Recurring drought, a normal situation for the area, resulted in famine, which was exacerbated by political instability and difficulties in transporting produce to market. A massive refugee movement from the province of Tigre (also spelled Tigray) to other parts of Ethiopia and neighboring countries was the outcome (Druce and Hammond 1990).

Rural women in refugee situations continue to face their traditional tasks of feeding and caring for their families and must often attempt to fulfill their roles under severe circumstances. They may lack male protection and may be particularly vulnerable to physical and sexual abuse. They often have little or no access to food, water, medical facilities, or shelter. While an asylum country or the international aid community may see refugees as a temporary problem, some displaced persons may never return to their country of origin and may thus need assistance for permanent resettlement in new and initially unfamiliar areas. Women in such circumstances have the same needs for land, water, credit, extension services, and training that local women have; their status as refugees simply exacerbates the problems they face (Wallace 1991b).

Martin (1991) emphasizes that refugee populations can be a positive force in their new locations if resources are targeted for them. Refugees may bring new ideas and skills to the host country, and their presence may bring more international development funding targeted at poor populations. Taft (1987:35) outlines major areas of need developed by the Refugee Policy Group and directed toward relief agencies working with refugees.

They are (1) a family focus for services to refugees, (2) the need for a broader base of knowledge regarding refugee women, and (3) a strengthening of institutions that serve refugees.

Long-term development strategies are needed to deal effectively with issues involving refugees and forced migrants. More information is needed regarding the effects of government policies and development programs intended to stem the flow of migration from rural to urban areas and from Third World to First World countries. Finally, programs designed to increase opportunities and options in rural areas must include women as active participants if improvements in living conditions are to occur.

Part II

Applications of the Gender-Focused
Approach to Special Project Areas

9

LIVESTOCK MANAGEMENT

Judith Warner and Ellen Hansen

In many world societies, women and men specialize in caring for particular types of animals (Chavangi and Hanssen 1983; Dahl 1987; Gauch and David 1983; Safilios-Rothschild 1983). Ownership of livestock is a sign of wealth and prestige in many societies, and control over livestock and dairy products provides women with important sources of household food and income (Feuerstein, Shaw, and Lovel 1987; Watson-Franke 1987).

A study in Bangladesh (Feldman, Banu, and McCarthy 1986) details the resources obtainable from livestock: animals provide 98 percent of draft power in agriculture; skin and hides are important exports; and dung is essential in fertilizing crops and is a widely used building material. In return, by-products from women's agricultural production are important sources of food for household animals (Oxby 1991). Because livestock is a capital asset and is nutritionally useful for women and their families, project planners must carefully assess women's activities in pastoralist and mixed farming systems in order to implement successful livestock development programs.

THE GENDER DIVISION OF LABOR

The gender division of labor varies cross-culturally and geographically by type of animal. Even where men are chiefly responsible for herding, women have responsibilities for dairying, food processing, or the use of animal by-products, and women generally own and care for small animals such as pigs, rabbits, guinea pigs, and chickens (Feuerstein, Shaw, and Lovel

1987; Paris 1989a; Peters 1986; Swift 1991). Careful evaluation is required to determine the extent of women's participation in livestock management and production. In a crop-and-livestock project in the Philippines, household records did not show women as active producers, although field observations revealed that they were. Project directors discovered that men were keeping the records and tended to consider their wives' work in livestock production as an extension of their household chores (Paris 1989b). The following section describes some commonalities and differences observed in Third World countries in the gender division of labor for livestock management.

Cattle

Women's responsibilities in cattle care and the processing of by-products vary by type of farming system and location. In mixed farming systems in Third World countries, where crop farming and livestock production are combined, women's work often involves tending and feeding cattle as well as dairying (Chavangi and Hanssen 1983; Paris 1989a). Other activities commonly performed by women in cattle-raising societies include cutting and carrying fodder, collecting dung for fuel, herding cattle based near the household, and milking.

In African pastoralist societies, cattle herding tends to be a male activity, while women are involved in dairying and related food-processing (Chavangi and Hanssen 1983; Weinpahl 1984), although this varies within regions and even within communities. In Nigeria, for example, milking is done by Twareg men (Oxby 1991). In Mongolia, both women and men herd cattle and yaks, but women are responsible for most milk processing, which generates income for much of the country's population (Swift 1991). On the island of Granada in the Caribbean, women rarely own or tend cattle (Brierley 1993), while in the Andes of Peru, women have historically been tenders and milkers of cows (Deere 1990).

A study of a village in Bangladesh revealed that women in nearly all the households surveyed (70 of 74) participated in cattle production in addition to raising chickens, ducks, and goats (Begum 1989). A complex leasing system allows women from low-income, nonlandholding households to supplement their income by caring for other households' animals. In the Guajiro society of Colombia and Venezuela, where men do most or all of the herding, animals are owned by women and men, and men do not have control over the cattle or by-products owned by their wives (Watson-Franke 1987).

Small Ruminants

Women's role in caring for sheep and goats is also variable. Small ruminants tend to be "women's animals" in many sub-Saharan African countries and in the Andean region of South America (Brydon and Chant 1989; Okali and Sumberg 1986; Safilios-Rothschild 1983; Watson-Franke 1987). African women own sheep and goats, and their children often have the responsibility for herding (Kettel 1989). Women's responsibilities vary within regions, however. Somali women manage cattle, sheep, goats, and sometimes camels because they and their children are the ones who drink the milk produced (Niamir 1990). In the Caribbean, women generally prefer small animals, but in some areas they also care for cows and horses, especially in regions of significant male out-migration (Brierley 1993:200; Harry 1993:214). Women are able to combine caring for sheep and goats with gardening and food processing, using kitchen waste and food by-products as feed for their small animals (Okali and Sumberg 1986). When properly managed, goats provide a source of milk year-round and are a valuable resource in hard times (Cloud 1986).

Other Small Animals

Women tend, feed, sell, and use the products of a variety of small animals, including chickens, turkeys, ducks, guinea fowl, rabbits, and other traditional or nontraditional small livestock (Cloud 1986; Gauch and David 1983; Kettel 1989). These animals require a minimum of care and scavenge for food on their own, with the exception of rabbits, which must be penned and require feeding. Gauch and David (1983) note that women keep small animals for household consumption, sales, ritual sacrifices, hospitality meals, manure, and commercial production. Small animals are especially important to women because they are a source of income generally under women's control.

Dairying

Throughout the Third World, women are the primary dairy producers and processors of related by-products for home consumption or local sale (Chavangi 1983). Zimmerman (1982) found that, in Egypt, women's household economic work includes tending animals, providing fodder, milking, and making cheese and butter. Niamir (1990) notes that among the Fulani of Nigeria, women's work with animals is limited to milking (for a detailed discussion of women's role in pastoral Fulani society, see Dupire 1960). Women in other pastoral groups, however, have the primary responsibility for management and decision making regarding herd animals because they and their children consume the milk produced (see also Netting 1993). Among the Sheikhanzai of Afghanistan, women do not herd animals but are responsible for dairying and processing wool or hair products (Tavakolian 1987). Tubu women of Chad herd, water, and milk cattle, providing one of two staples of the daily diet, which consists of milk and millet (Baroin 1987).

Selection of New Livestock Species

Projects seeking to introduce new breeds or varieties of animals to women need to consider women's level of involvement in livestock production within a particular society. For example, if small ruminants are introduced into a culture in which caring for small livestock is a man's activity, women may face social constraints on their participation in management. In Kenya, a livestock project supplied goats to village-level women's organizations to be kept in screened shelters. Because goats were considered men's responsibility and cultural norms dictated that women did not stay out at night to guard property, the project hired men as herders and watchmen. Women, however, did such time-consuming tasks as carrying forage, providing water in the dry season, and milking the goats. Although the project had anticipated that the cooperatively owned stall goats would provide income for women, men continued to make economic decisions about the sale or slaughter of the animals, and no direct economic benefits appeared to accrue to women from the project (Noble and Nolan 1983).

An important step, being practiced more and more by development planners, is listening to and involving the people who will be affected by any project from the very beginning of the planning process. Another is to base any project, including the introduction of new animal species, on local knowledge and needs (see Ladipo 1991; Stamp 1990). Cloud (1986) listened to women in Mali and Senegal express their needs regarding livestock: they wanted improved breeds of chickens and goats for crossbreeding with their own animals. In Nigeria, women requested a particular breed of goat valued for its red skin as an income-generating export.

TIME ALLOCATION

As is highlighted throughout this volume, women's days are filled with work. Project planners considering the introduction of new animals must obtain accurate information regarding women's time constraints in order to avoid making additional demands on their already heavy work schedules.

Women usually are responsible for cutting and carrying fodder for animals that are not free-grazers. Stall feeding (in which fodder is carried to the animals) and creep-feeding (in which animals are confined to corrals that are moved regularly) can greatly increase women's workload (Chavangi and Hanssen 1983). A Malian livestock project controlled the mating of small ruminants, which led to a concentration of births in the rainy season when women were involved in dryland agriculture. This created a time conflict between milking, cheese-making, and necessary agricultural work (Carloni 1982, cited in Safilios-Rothschild 1983).

Because women are the major food preparers and processors in many Third World regions, they often use the wastes from these activities to feed small ruminants. In Nigeria, many more women keep goats than sheep, as the goats tend to stay close to the homestead, allowing women to take advantage of the availability of kitchen wastes and food processing by-products to feed their animals (Okali and Sumberg 1986).

Kettel (1989) points out that African women's activities in cattle herding are daily tasks, including carrying fodder, watering the animals, and milking. Men's duties, in contrast, may be more difficult or more dangerous (bleeding, castrating, and moving animals to new pastures, for example) but do not necessarily require daily involvement with and time expenditures on their animals.

OWNERSHIP OF LIVESTOCK PRODUCTION RESOURCES

In many societies, women own small ruminants and poultry (Dahl 1987; Gauch and David 1983; Okali and Sumberg 1986), and as noted above, women generally retain control of income derived from dairying. In some areas of Africa, women may inherit or purchase small numbers of cattle (Echbal 1981, cited in Safilios-Rothschild 1983). However, women's ownership of small ruminants and cattle is often not independent of their husbands, and women must ask permission if they wish to sell an animal. Henderson (1980, 1986) interviewed women of the semisedentary Fulani group in Burkina Faso, three-quarters of whom indicated that they had received cows from their relatives, while one-quarter had been given cows by their husbands. The cows are kept with the herds of the women's husbands or male relatives. The women consider cattle a form of capital, but in order to sell an animal, they require permission from the man in whose herd the animal is kept (see also Dupire 1960). Talle (1988) describes the complex system of ownership and control of cattle practiced by the Masai of Kenya, where women have use rights to cattle but cannot sell or slaughter them. Watson (1991) presents a similar situation among the Turkana of Kenya, where women control animal products but men make decisions regarding livestock management and control cash income.

A lack of draft power, or the lack of a male in the household with access to cattle, is a major reason women-headed households in mixed farming systems are unable to plow fields to plant crops. A study by Peters (1986) indicates that while women who own cattle are sometimes involved in plowing, more often they must wait until a male relative is available to help. Households that do not own cattle depend on links with other households and are thus vulnerable to exchange demands and delays in planting. With their restricted rights of property ownership, women are particularly vulnerable to these constraints.

INCOME GENERATION

Livestock Production

In spite of their increasing involvement in caring for livestock in mixed farming systems (Burton, White, and Dow 1982; Spring, Smith, and Kayuni 1983), women are seldom selected as participants in large livestock projects. In the Lilongwe Rural Development Project, a stall-feeding project in Malawi, men were recruited by extension workers or through training classes (Spring 1986). Women were rarely contacted directly, and received no extension assistance in participating in stall-feeding activities. Women became involved in stall feeding through the participation of their husbands, which resulted in wives obtaining steers for a joint enterprise; husband-initiated stall feeding, which led to the wife's involvement even after the husband had left the program; and by their own efforts. Not surprisingly, self-initiated women's ventures are started more frequently in areas where other women are already participating in a program. Women have had to approach the project themselves in order to get attention. Self-initiating women have had to make a greater investment in the stall-feeding project than men, often taking out loans or engaging in nonagricultural work such as beer-brewing to finance these enterprises.

The Malawi stall-feeding project provides an example of a successful venture for women, but it also demonstrates culturally prescribed spending allocations. Because women have less access to cash, they have had to use their profits to purchase family necessities, such as food and clothing, instead of being able to invest in housing or cattle, or saving it (Spring 1986).

Small-Ruminant Production

Sheep and goats are often viewed as appropriate animals for women's projects aimed at raising family living standards rather than generating income. This perception may be in part because women's small-ruminant projects have seldom generated income (Safilios-Rothschild 1983). Okali and Sumberg (1986) point out, however, that individual women (and men) in western Africa own goats, which could generate income sufficient to provide capital for investment in development. In addition, small animals provide a relatively dependable source of food throughout the year for women and their families (Cloud 1986) and can be an important source of income in the form of mobile capital for women in the event of divorce (Safilios-Rothschild 1983).

A vital element of any project in small-ruminant production is women's participation as owners and managers of the animals. Projects providing inputs for female-managed small-ruminant components may be attractive to women seeking new sources of personal income. Women in a Philippine village, for example, raise pigs for sale to generate income to pay their children's tuition fees and to finance inputs into their rice farms. They also pay hired laborers on their farms in kilos of swine rather than in scarce cash (Paris 1989a).

Livestock Projects and Dairying

The sale of dairy products locally is an important source of income for women in both semisedentary pastoralist and mixed farming systems. In Egypt, women sell butter and cheese and use the profits to buy food and nonfood items such as clothing for themselves and their children. Milk products are also used as in-kind payments for laborers working on family fields and as support and gifts to family members residing outside the immediate family residence. The small sums produced regularly during the milking season provide income to meet daily household needs, to maintain social networks, and to help the poor (Zimmerman 1982).

In Burkina Faso, married Fulani women have usufruct rights as well as ownership in cows, and they decide how to use the milk. Women tend to keep a portion of the milk for their family and to sell the rest, using the money for family and personal use. Adult men are viewed as the herd owners and managers, while adult women are the dairy producers and milk vendors. The income women gain through marketing dairy products contributes substantially to aggregate household income (Henderson 1980; Horowitz 1979).

The position of women in herding societies is threatened by the objectives of productivity-oriented projects that seek to convert the local economy from one that depends on dairy production for rural consumption to one that emphasizes meat production for external markets (Horowitz 1979; Kettel 1989; Thiam 1991). Projects focused on increasing productivity often emphasize limiting herd size and conserving milk for better nutrition for fewer calves. This policy can have a negative impact on family nutrition due to decreased milk consumption and a reduction in women's income from dairying activities. In areas where herding societies do not practice agriculture, the exchange of milk for grain is a major source of basic cereals for the family. Where decreased milk consumption leads to increased amounts of grains in the household diet, women's workload increases correspondingly, as milk requires relatively less preparation time than grain (Kettel 1989).

Dairy production not only provides a source of income for women, it is also an important component of the social structure of both sedentary and nomadic groups (Dahl 1987; Kettel 1989; Talle 1987, 1988; Tavakolian 1987). The authors cited describe the exchange networks women establish to share labor, animals, and products, which also lead to greater autonomy and prestige for them within their households and communities. Any development project that deals with livestock production must be built on an understanding not only of livestock management practices but also of the social networks that maintain them. In projects that emphasize the commercial production of beef, aggregate household income may increase while women's income declines. Loss of control over dairy sales or access to cows for dairy production can decrease women's influence in family decision making (Vaidyanathan 1983).

High rates of calf mortality under semi-arid range conditions in Africa have been attributed in part to competition for milk between calves and pastoralist communities. In the rainy season, sufficient milk is available for all needs, but milk availability varies throughout the year, depending on management practices and herd size (Kettel 1989; Stenning 1959; Talle 1988). Seasonality is important in management practices in Mongolia, where the climate dictates that animal births take place in one short period each year. Herdswomen who manage milk production have developed methods of converting milk into forms that can be stored for long periods, such as dried curds, yogurt, and fermented milk (Swift 1991).

Livestock Marketing

In cases where raising small animals is promoted as an income-generating activity, planners need to consider women's activities in the marketing sector and take them into account when designing projects. Although women are generally the primary owners of small animals, they often have a lesser role than do men in decisions concerning sales and the marketing of sheep and goats (Dahl 1987; Safilios-Rothschild 1983). In West Africa, where women are very active in trading, a majority of livestock traders are men. In some societies, however, such as in Togo, women dominate small-ruminant trading (Josserand and Ariza-Niño 1982).

Women of the Tubu of northern Africa tend young animals, milk cows, and sometimes camels, and water the herds. Taking animals to market is men's work, as women are not able to travel far from home because of their labor obligations (Baroin 1987). In Bangladesh, according to social custom, rural women do not assume roles in business and therefore have no control over, and little knowledge of, the workings of the market. They are active in livestock production and dairying, but their participation in buying and selling is severely limited (Begum 1989).

Among the Masai of Kenya, increasing poverty has led people to sell cattle that were previously considered the subsistence base of the household. Thus the cattle are seen as "marketable versus procreative animals" (Talle 1987:75). This change has had various negative impacts on women's positions because animals are sold for cash, which is often controlled by men.

Dairy Marketing

As discussed above, milk production is usually an activity controlled by women, and the sale of dairy products is an important source of income for women. Dahl (1987) notes that women's control over dairy products is ultimately mediated through the men, who own the animals, thus constraining women's abilities to distribute food and market milk surpluses.

Kettel (1989) recommends the development of small-scale, women-run dairies to heighten women's roles in their communities through an activity that is culturally appropriate and that provides a product that enjoys continuing demand. She points out, however, that women's productive work in dairying has tended to be considered part of their domestic chores rather than an important and integral part of livestock management.

Women often walk long distances to sell milk or milk products (Chavangi and Hanssen 1983), or they must wait for long periods for milk buyers to come to them (Chavangi 1983). In spite of these limitations, dairy marketing holds great potential for economic development for both women and men.

Commercial Dairying

The commercialization of dairying activities has been successful for Mongolian herdswomen, and demand for milk products has increased recently as the country's economy has opened up. Traditional dairy products are made by women, who stand to benefit from increasing demand for the products (Swift 1991).

In contrast, changes in northwestern Jordan have adversely affected women. The commercialization of milk and egg production has led to an increase in sales and a decrease in home processing primarily for home consumption. Families purchase commercially processed foods, which often have been poorly stored and have become depleted of nutrients by the time of purchase. Although rural Jordanian women's food processing is a time-consuming task, the value to the small householder of replacing traditional foods with commercial ones is questionable (Basson 1981).

In many instances, the rise of a modern dairying industry has created more work for women while depriving them of income. Chavangi (1983) reports that 80 percent of Kenyan milk yield is produced in the small-farm sector and estimates that women contribute 85 percent of the labor. However, only women heads of households receive direct compensation for their efforts; the bulk of women involved in dairying are unpaid family laborers. In this situation, Chavangi and Hanssen (1983) point out that providing price incentives for increasing milk production will fail to motivate those who actually do the work.

Referring to the Sudan, Badri (1986, cited in Kettel 1989) suggests that small-scale dairies run by women could save the country millions of dollars in yearly milk imports. Creating dairying cooperatives does not necessarily ensure that women will benefit directly, however. Payments for milk, which were traditionally given to women members of a Gujarat cooperative, were generally claimed by men when families joined the cooperative (Chavangi and Hanssen 1983). In part, this was due to the fact that men formally owned the cattle and were official cooperative members. In families that belonged to the cooperative, 50 percent of the total family income came from dairying, compared to only 20 percent in families that did not belong. Men controlled the increased income from selling through the cooperative, and because their purchasing priorities were different from women's, they tended to spend the income on nonfood items. Many families, especially the poorest, sold most of their milk and dairy products and purchased food of lower nutritional value; thus their nutritional state actually declined (Chavangi and Hanssen 1983).

In order to direct income to women through commercial dairying enterprises, women must be involved as producers. By building on traditional gender roles, project planners can maintain dairying as an income-generating activity for women, and commercial dairy projects can be designed to accommodate women's needs. Additional research is required to gather information regarding women's work in dairying (Dahl 1987; Kettel 1989).

CREDIT

Women have seldom been the primary targets of livestock credit programs. In the steer stall-raising program in Malawi described above, men were the project's targets (Spring 1986). Women initiated efforts to join the project on their own but found it difficult to receive credit. Spring writes that women had to convince the agents that they were creditworthy and were often told that, to be eligible, they had to form a group. In essence, the system is organized to process credit to men, who are individually issued steers, while women have had to gain acceptance by the extension staff before they are allowed to join.

In a crop-and-livestock project in the Philippines, men have access through banks to credit for purchasing livestock (Paris 1989a). Through the National Food Authority (NFA), men participating in the project can sell rice at a higher price than at the market. Women, who rarely have the necessary collateral, do not borrow at the bank or the NFA; rather, they use informal loan sources and pay higher interest rates. Only people with accounts at the NFA can take advantage of either the higher price offered for rice or the other project benefits, such as low-interest loans. Women as well as men have access to low-interest, no-collateral loans through the farmers' association if they are members, but few are.

Extending credit to women must be based on a solid local infrastructure. Goat raising has been a popular form of experimental women's project (Safilios-Rothschild 1983), yet despite the emphasis on organizing women, extending credit, and promoting women's income-generating activities, women have had difficulty in maintaining control of such projects. In a project in southern Ethiopia, for example, a local women's association was granted interest-free loans to purchase goats and set up stalls (Bekele 1982, cited in Safilios-Rothschild 1983). In the start-up phase, women cared for the animals, but as the scheme began to appear profitable, the local men's cooperative set up a committee to oversee the project and took over herding. Although this incursion was presented as a reciprocal act to compensate women for their agricultural labor, women's control over the project was eroded.

Safilios-Rothschild (1983) notes that women's lack of formal organizational skills in management and leadership places them at a disadvantage. In Ethiopia, plans were made to train women in cooperative skills and reintegrate them into the goat-raising scheme. Safilios-Rothschild recommends that all rural women who participate in livestock projects receive training in credit transactions; bookkeeping, managerial, organizational, and cooperative skills; and marketing techniques.

Flora and Santos (1986) report on a livestock project in the Dominican Republic in which women receive "credit in kind." A pregnant milk cow is given to each woman who has been trained in raising tethered cows on the condition that the calf be returned to the project for distribution to other women participants. By 1983 the project had distributed more than seventy cows but had received only three calves in return. Flora and Santos advise that more time is needed to determine if the rate of return on these "loans" will improve.

Collateral is generally required for formal loans from established banks. Paris (1989a) notes that banks in the Philippines would accept only livestock or a land title as collateral—requirements that leave most women out. Even widows who owned livestock in their own names had to have a guarantor in order to borrow money from the bank. A new plan established in Uganda requires that farmers be "full-time cultivators, bona fide residents of their area, regular taxpayers and owners of basic property such as houses or animals" (Morna et al. 1990b:30). Women farmers and pastoralists often meet the first two requirements but rarely meet the last two, so the credit plan remains out of their reach.

A livestock project in India targeted women in households involved in dairying (Rutherford 1987). Initially the program had little success, partly because of the poverty and risk aversion of the participants and partly because of poor management practices and low productivity. Project planners and women participants jointly discussed these problems and made major changes in the program to improve it. They established para-veterinary training seminars for women, some of them illiterate, who now practice in their villages. Administrators and participants learned that "a cattle loan in itself may not necessarily benefit, and might even adversely affect, poor women. . . . Without training and follow-up, a cattle loan may not be productive" (Rutherford 1987:249).

APPROPRIATE TECHNOLOGY

Appropriate technology in livestock management may include modern machinery, as in the case of the dairy described below, or it may mean animals for draft power or transport in agricultural areas where human beings have traditionally provided the labor. Especially where mechanical technology is not feasible because of high costs for fuel and machinery, draft animals may be the most appropriate technology for both women and men. Using animals to carry water and fuelwood lightens women's workload. Similarly, introducing draft animals such as oxen, donkeys, or camels may allow women farmers to work their fields more efficiently.

Introducing draft animals requires sensitivity on the part of project planners. Adequate food must be available to feed the animals at critical times of the year, especially for pregnant and lactating animals; implements to be used must be appropriate to the type of animal available; traditions prohibiting women's use of animals must be taken into account before any project is initiated; the cost of the animals and any tools must be within reach of project participants; and physical conditions, such as the existence of animal diseases or prohibitive terrain, must be considered (Pearson 1991; Stamp 1990).

Medical technology to improve animal health has been successfully introduced in Africa (Pearson 1991), but schemes for range management and controlled restocking have been less successful (Wiggins 1991). Thiam (1991) describes a restocking scheme implemented by the government in northern Mali that disregarded the people's traditional livestock practices, which the authorities saw as destructive and inefficient. Predictably, the plan failed because it introduced new breeds of cattle not adapted to the area and ignored the needs and traditions of the people affected by the changes. As Pearson (1991:14) points out, "It is usually the simplest idea or design that is the most successful, . . . as it is the one that can be most easily adopted."

An Egyptian dairy project established a cooperative with a milk separator that was operated by a local woman hired to assist in dairy production and to work with village women. To improve hygiene in processing the milk, the project developed lectures on hygiene and encouraged the women to use a new, quicker-acting starter and cheese cloths to replace the mats on which the cheese traditionally had been drained (Henderson 1985). Village women were not enthusiastic about the hygiene lessons but came in order to be able to use the separator. Since the beginning of the project, however, more privately owned separators have been installed in the village, and consequently demand has lessened for the project's machine even though the unit cost of using the latter was lower than that of the privately owned separators. Distance and time are important factors to village women and override the lower prices charged by the project dairy.

EXTENSION AND TRAINING

Livestock extension efforts targeted to women are critically needed (Morna et al. 1990a; Safilios-Rothschild 1983; see also Chap. 7). In the past, women have seldom had access to veterinary extension information and medical advice because of a lack of trained women veterinary technicians and extension agents. In Cloud's (1986) visits with African women's groups, she frequently heard of women's desire for paraprofessional and professional training in animal husbandry and agriculture.

Kantara (1986) describes a project in Mali that was centered around participation of the pastoral people in the area, particularly women. Training for local people, at the time of Kantara's report, was an effort in transition and experimentation. Project planners were working with local women to hear and incorporate their concerns and needs in livestock management and were changing the program accordingly. The important aspect of this project was that planners recognized the relevance and applicability to development of women's knowledge and skills.

Women's small-livestock raising has seldom been a focus of extension work. Gauch and David (1983) point out that extension agents may not want to devote their careers to providing advice on low-prestige and low-profit animals such as poultry and rabbits. Because small animals tend to be free-ranging, providing health care for them is more time-consuming and is often incompletely implemented. However, African women who met with Cloud (1986) expressed a strong interest in improving breeds of small animals, including chickens and goats (Cloud 1986). Because small animals are generally owned and controlled by women, extension services and training in their care are of interest and concern to them.

OUT-MIGRATION

Male out-migration often greatly increases women's workload in both livestock raising and agriculture. In Botswana, for example, high out-migration of men from some villages has left the tasks of livestock management and plowing with cattle to women (Brown 1981; Fortmann 1980; Peters 1986), while at the same time the absence of men leaves women with limited access to animals for plowing and a lack of male labor. When men are absent, women must take on traditionally male tasks such as watering the animals, moving them to new pastures daily or seasonally, and arranging for breeding and medical care. Traditional systems of livestock management and agriculture that dealt successfully with changing physical and social conditions are currently undergoing intense economic and environmental pressure and change. Male out-migration for work is one response to such pressures, resulting in corresponding changes in women's lives as well (see Chap. 8).

COMMUNITY PLANNING

In this volume we have cited many examples of projects that have failed after being initiated without the participation of local people, especially women. Working with existing women's groups or helping to establish new ones can be one way to facilitate community involvement in development projects. In Burkina Faso, for example, women of three ethnic groups organized a livestock committee (Henderson 1986). Committee members had their chickens vaccinated and mobilized their husbands to build a poultry-breeding unit for an improved breed. After considerable delay, the donor-funded project delivered the new breed of chicken, but the animals died within a few months because the imported breed of chicken selected was not suitable for the harsh local conditions.

The development literature is replete with sad stories of projects that started with good intentions and failed to achieve their goals or actually worsened the quality of life for project participants. Strong community

involvement from conception to implementation is vital to any development project. Including women in the process as community representatives is crucial to the success of the project and to the advancement of
women. Thiam's (1991) report from northern Mali (described above) is a
telling reminder of what can happen when planners do not work closely
with the women and men of the communities they will affect. Kantara's
(1986) enthusiastic description of a livestock project that involves the entire community and its needs is an example from the opposite end of the
spectrum, an indication that, with sensitive planning and the appropriate
application of technology and other inputs, crop and livestock projects can
have a positive impact on the lives of the people they are intended to assist.

10

WATER MANAGEMENT

Judith Warner and Ellen Hansen

In a time of concern over the world's agricultural and domestic water supply, women constitute an important target group for water project planning (Cloud 1984; Roark 1980). Water supply improvements have received increasing national and donor government investment, but uneven access to inputs for men and women has lowered productivity and increased inequality within households and communities and between socioeconomic levels (Turner and Suizo 1986). Project inputs directed toward women are necessary because of women's significant involvement in agricultural production and household water use. In most regions, women are active in both irrigated and rain-fed (or dryland) farming, especially in such labor-intensive activities as planting, weeding, and harvesting (Carr 1991; Dixon 1982; Dixon-Mueller 1985). Throughout the Third World, women and girls have responsibilities for household water provision and use (Black 1990; Dankelman and Davidson 1988; UN Water Conference 1977), and in some areas women spend as much as eight hours a day fetching water (INSTRAW 1989a). Gender issues are key elements in any water development project, and planners must be concerned with women's roles in water use as farmers, agricultural laborers, and household suppliers and consumers.

Projects that fail to target women directly may inadvertently change women's work patterns, creating serious labor bottlenecks that negatively impact women's income-generating and household activities (Burfisher and Horenstein 1985; Dey 1981; Jackson 1985) and agricultural production in general (Moris and Thom 1990; Ogbe 1989). For women's roles and needs to be addressed adequately in water projects, data regarding the gender division of labor and household resource allocation patterns must be available to project planners. Consulting with women and including them in water users' associations are important aspects of project planning (INSTRAW 1989b).

THE GENDER DIVISION OF LABOR

Women's Role in Irrigated and Rain-Fed Farming

In all regions of the world, women participate in agricultural production to some degree (Dankelman and Davidson 1988; Dixon 1982; Dixon-Mueller 1985; UN 1991). Women may specialize in kitchen gardens or cash cropping, small-animal raising or tree crops. Successful water projects necessarily include research on gender roles to determine the division of labor in irrigated and rain-fed farming, noting whether women and men specialize in particular crops and the degree to which household members conduct their activities as joint or separate enterprises (Guyer 1980; Moris and Thom 1990). Inputs to water projects have often been directed to male heads of households, resulting in adverse impacts on intrahousehold labor and resource allocation because project planners have often assumed that water system improvements will uniformly benefit all household members (Cloud 1984).

Irrigation water is often provided for the development of cash crops rather than subsistence crops. Therefore control is often vested in the male head of household, who is more likely to be involved in cash cropping. As a result, traditional gender-based patterns of crop ownership and work responsibilities are overlooked. In The Gambia, for example, rice was traditionally a woman's private crop. Women provided the labor and used the crop for both personal income and household consumption. They gained access to rice land through usufruct or communal land rights (Carney and Watts 1991; Dey 1985). Projects to improve rice production in The Gambia have undermined women's independent production, however, by assigning the right to irrigated land to male heads of households, by failing to extend credit or new technologies to women, by creating time conflicts between work designed to intensify rice production and that needed to tend dry-land crops or other income-generating activities; and by failing to include independent female rice producers in the market structure of a modernizing Gambia (Dey 1985).

After community irrigation projects failed in the 1960s and 1970s, the Gambian government introduced large-scale irrigation in the mid-1980s. Women were specifically targeted in the Jahaly Pacharr project, but project planners and managers failed to consider adequately the traditional social aspects of the household division of labor, land rights, and the control of resources and produce. When the project did not result in increased production on fields worked cooperatively by men and women, women took steps to protest changes that had led to men's increasing control over the rice production. Women also made the best of a bad situation: those who lost independent access to irrigated lands formed labor groups to work in the irrigated rice fields for pay. By working in groups, they earned more money than by working individually as day laborers (Carney and Watts 1991).

Women as Procurers of Domestic Water

Women in all parts of the Third World are responsible for providing and managing water for domestic use (Black 1990; INSTRAW 1989a and 1989b; Rodda 1991). As these duties have become more difficult because of declining water tables, changes in land use and tenure, and other factors, women have become increasingly involved in projects to provide safe drinking water in their communities (Black 1990; INSTRAW 1989a and 1989b). For example, in the mid-1980s, the Grameen Bank in Bangladesh provided tube wells as part of a drinking water program. By 1987 more than 1,500 people had applied for the wells, and more than two-thirds of the applicants were landless women who were already members of the Grameen Bank (Black 1990). In Guinea-Bissau, older respected women were trained as promoters to encourage other villagers to use a safe water source. Planners also acknowledged women's interest in small-scale vegetable growing and developed a project to supply irrigation water as well as drinking water (INSTRAW 1989b).

When women are prohibited from decision making within their households and men decide to participate in development projects or build homes according to their own priorities, household water needs may not be taken into account. Thus women, who know where water sources are located and when water is available, often have not had input into decisions that greatly affect their lives (Dankelman and Davidson 1988). Mathew (1991) cites an example of a chicken farming project in Zaire. Women were not consulted about the project, which required the procurement of significant amounts of fresh water and therefore added time demands to women's already busy days.

Access to fresh water for drinking and other domestic uses has been affected by drought and desertification, dam building that displaces rural people, irrigation projects that redirect water to new uses and contaminate it with salts and chemicals, and industrial development that pollutes formerly clean water sources (Black 1990; Robson 1991; Rodda 1991; World Bank 1990). Where women have been consulted about water projects and have become involved in the care and maintenance of water systems, evidence shows that they are effective and responsible managers (Black 1990; Dankelman and Davidson 1988; INSTRAW 1989b).

TIME ALLOCATION

Water projects that facilitate crop intensification may increase the need for women's agricultural labor (Burfisher and Horenstein 1985; Carney and Watts 1991). This situation may benefit women if they receive a wage and/or a portion of the crop for household use or personal sale, but costly labor bottlenecks can result. When newly irrigated crops are placed under the control of men but women are made responsible for intensive tasks, women may see the new labor as a time-consuming burden. Increased agricultural work can conflict with women's subsistence or private cropping and household tasks (child care and food processing, for example), resulting in diminishing returns for women and lowered productivity. Rice farming projects provide one example of how directing resource inputs toward men can negatively affect women's time allocations. Moris and Thom (1990) suggest that the amount of labor a rural African woman is willing to contribute to her husband's irrigated crops depends on what the husband is willing to pay.

   Irrigation projects that give control of new plots to men can fail to realize production goals because of a reduced commitment from women (Carney and Watts 1991; Dey 1981). In The Gambia, women were required to work on their husbands' rice paddies with or without compensation, which greatly increased their workload and reduced the time available for their own income-generating activities. Under these circumstances, women responded by partially withdrawing their labor. Dey's (1981) study of three Gambian irrigation projects found that in the dry season, when women had few income-earning activities, they were very willing to work on their husbands' fields. However, in the rainy season, when women grew rice, a critical labor shortage occurred. Women preferred working on their own fields and would work on men's fields only on days when they were not active on their own. This resulted in delayed transplanting and weeding. The overall result was lowered productivity because many men chose not to grow rainy-season rice due to the shortage of female labor and the necessity of paying a wage to farm workers (Carney and Watts 1991).

In a case from northern Cameroon, Jones (1982) notes that decreasing the level of return for women by placing rice under male control can lower family productivity. Although women received cash and a portion of the crop for working on their husbands' rice fields, they preferred to work on their own sorghum fields. Providing individual irrigated plots for women and greater compensation for hired female laborers would be a direct method of dealing with these production constraints.

Cash Crops and Time Allocation

A major gender issue that has emerged from analyses of water projects concerns the changing prioritization of irrigated and rain-fed agriculture. An increased emphasis on irrigated cash crops can create time allocation conflicts with rain-fed subsistence crops, which are often women's responsibility. In Sri Lanka, a major resettlement scheme attempted to replace all dryland subsistence crops with irrigated ones (Benson and Emmert 1985). Although women had contributed substantial labor in both paddy and dryland agriculture, they were not given many work tasks on the mechanized irrigated plots. As a result, women's labor was underutilized during the period when they normally would have tended dryland crops and was insufficient during the peak season for irrigated agriculture. Families suffered because they were deprived of the nutritious dryland crops (finger millet, grains, pulses, and vegetables) that women had previously produced.

The Kano River Irrigation Project in Nigeria serves as another example of how project modification of local cropping systems can lower family productivity (Jackson 1985). The Kano River Project's goals were to increase the food supply, generate employment opportunities, and improve the standard of living. Jackson suggests that another, implicit goal of the project was to transform the subsistence economy into a modern market system. Wheat and tomatoes were introduced as cash crops to support urban bakeries and a tomato paste factory. At no point in project planning were women's needs considered; therefore no activities were included to meet them.

After the project was implemented, the goal of increasing the food supply was derailed by local food deficits related to declining availability of traditional subsistence crops: sorghum, millet, beans, and cassava. The decline was generated by the displacement of 28 percent of female and 33 percent of male farmers from their land, increased pests and weeds due to the presence of a year-round water supply, failure to use all available irrigated land because of the high cost of labor and inputs, and time conflicts between irrigated and dryland agriculture. Despite initial adversity, however, some Muslim Hausa women were able to benefit from the new situation through their own initiative. Because they had traditionally been compensated in grain for labor on their husbands' crops, they were able to increase crop sales and develop a snack food business. In contrast, non–Muslim Hausa women were not remunerated for agricultural labor on family fields and undertook increased work on their husbands' fields at the expense of their own crop production. Non–Muslim women's farms decreased in size and declined in yield, a problem intensified by the fact that they were allocated the poorest land (Jackson 1985).

Projects that alter local cropping patterns need to maintain a balance between cash crops and subsistence crops, and take care to avoid creating new demands for women's labor that over- or underutilize women at key times during the cropping season. Cash crop schemes should provide for ownership or compensated participation by women in both irrigated and rain-fed cropping.

Kin Networks and Time Allocation

If project planning does not take into account the need for household labor, the increased labor demands of irrigated agriculture can place stress on families. In a Sri Lankan resettlement project, nuclear families were relocated on newly irrigated land. The absence of helping kin increased women's child care duties, and husband-wife teams had difficulty coping with the peak-season workload. The project dealt with these time constraints by trying to relocate families in villages where women had kin (Benson and Emmert 1985).

ACCESS TO LAND

Irrigation projects have adversely affected women's access to land (Cloud 1984) because improvements in the water supply increase the value of land and can result in land redistribution that favors men. For example, the increasing price of land within the Senegal River Basin has displaced women from fields they had traditionally planted. In addition, male migrants have returned to take back pump-irrigated land that women were using (Cloud 1982).

When dam construction has forced farmers to leave their land, women have had to locate new sources of water for agriculture and domestic use in resettlement sites as well as finding available fertile land for subsistence crops. When land is submerged, trees used by women for a variety of purposes are lost. Newly landless men may migrate in search of work, leaving women as heads of households, with or without access to farmland. Women who fished in rivers may not have adequate equipment for fishing in newly created large reservoirs. Downstream from dams, women's productivity is affected as river flows decrease, flood patterns change, land is left exposed during dry seasons, and formerly reliable sources of drinking water disappear (Ogbe 1989).

The assertion of land rights by male heads of households and the privatization of land can negatively affect women's access to land and water. Water projects must include policy objectives that provide for women's traditional land use and inheritance rights and that include women as members of water users' associations responsible for the reallocation of land (Turner and Suizo 1986).

WATER ALLOCATION

Access to water from project sources is an important gender issue. Women participate in making decisions about on-farm water use, yet project water sources have seldom been targeted for women's use unless the project is specifically aimed at the domestic water supply (Cloud 1984). Unfortunately, water projects that do not specifically provide water for women's use have benefited men to a far greater extent than women. When water pumps were introduced in the Senegal River Basin in Mauritania, for example, they were distributed to men, who operated them only in connection with their own agricultural production. Women had only seasonal access and in some cases had to hand-carry water from men's rice fields to their own private plots (Smale 1980). A similar situation arose in another area of Mauritania when vegetable gardens managed by women's cooperatives did not have sufficient access to water pumps. In many villages, women continued to hand-transport water from a river, pond, or well (Henderson 1989). Current project recommendations indicate that pumps should be made available to gardens close to the river and access to wells improved for distant gardens.

Cloud (1984) suggests that engineering changes in system design should emphasize creating sources of water for the homestead and women's private

or cooperative fields, providing domestic water for household use, and pre-
venting water-borne diseases.

Women in Water Management

One method for integrating women's concerns into water allocation planning is to involve women in the planning process directly. Women's influence in making decisions about labor-intensive activities is most significant
in those areas in which they are actively involved. Farm women in Dahod,
India, for example, are most involved with decision making regarding
planting, transplanting, and weeding. The most critical constraints affecting
women's agricultural production are timing and water quantity (Stanbury
1984).

Including women as members of water users' associations established by
a project ensures that women gain from participating in the project (Black
1990; INSTRAW 1989b; UN Water Conference 1977). Studies have shown that
women tend to have lower rates of participation in formal water users'
associations, but they often have informal roles in adjudicating water
disputes. Formalizing women's roles has proven beneficial for projects in
India, Sri Lanka, and the Philippines (Uphoff 1981, 1982a, 1982b, cited in
Cloud 1982).

As part of the Aslong communal irrigation project in the Philippines,
women were recognized as equal members of participating households
and were given joint membership responsibilities. Granting joint membership grew out of an acknowledgement of women's critical role in managing household budgets and in agricultural production and marketing.
Consulting with village women and careful scheduling of activities opened
the project to women's full participation in planning and implementation
(Illo 1988).

APPROPRIATE WATER TECHNOLOGY

Some irrigation projects have failed or have negatively affected women's
production because the technology applied was inappropriate to women's
social standing or needs. The small-scale irrigation schemes implemented
in The Gambia in the 1960s and 1970s, for example, were unsuccessful because women refused to work on irrigated plots controlled by men. Project planners had regarded village households as cohesive units whose

members all worked together for a common end (Carney and Watts 1991). Similarly, rice irrigation projects in Cameroon miscarried because planners did not consider that women would not work on their husbands' irrigated fields unless they earned a fair wage for their labor (Jones 1983, cited in Moris and Thom 1990).

A typical assumption on the part of development planners has been that rural women do not adopt new technologies because they are backward or ignorant (Stamp 1990). This position neglects issues that may seem unrelated to water supply but that are important to women. For example, an INSTRAW (1989b:3–4) report describes several water supply schemes that failed to address women's concerns:

> In rural Iran, communal laundry facilities built were large rectangular sinks, at adult waist height. However, Iranian women traditionally wash clothes and dishes in a squatting position. As a result, the laundry basins were not used. . . . Similarly, in Nicaragua, a latrine was not used by women because their feet could be seen from the outside. . . . [I]n some cultures women would not wish to wash themselves in full view of other villagers, and yet male engineers often place the pumps in the village square, thinking that was the most convenient location.

While the projects introduced technologies that seemed to be appropriate and that were designed to improve women's lives, important factors were not taken into account in project planning, so the projects did not have the expected results.

These examples illustrate that there is more to the concept of appropriate technology than installing hardware. Technology that appears to lighten women's workloads may be expropriated by men. In one case in Africa, for example, men took over the carts women had been given to carry water and firewood (Hoskins and Weber 1985). If placing a new technology, such as a public well in the center of a village, precludes women from participating in traditional social activities or private hygiene practices, women may not utilize it no matter how appropriate it may seem to be.

Providing adequate water for household use and home gardens or livestock strongly affects family well-being. Yet, although women are primarily responsible for procuring and utilizing household water, development agents have seldom contacted them about improvements in water supply and sanitation. Project planners have assumed that discussions with men about water use priorities are representative of household interests, but when men are consulted and women are not, an adequate domestic water supply is seldom given high priority (Elmendorf 1980; Elmendorf and Isely 1983). Because women procure most domestic water, projects that fail to provide for an adequate household water supply may inadvertently increase the amount of time women spend acquiring water and deprive them of time needed for other activities. No water system technology is appropriate if it is implemented without considering these issues.

Appropriate Traditional Technology

When planners disregard traditional methods in favor of new technologies, they run the risk of ignoring effective methods that have been used, sometimes for centuries, by rural people. As Hoskins and Weber write, "Introducing appropriate technologies is not new. Groups throughout the ages have shared or copied others' technologies when they found them appropriate. On the other hand, some groups living next to each other for centuries, in what appear to be similar situations, have rejected the others' tools, materials and techniques" (Hoskins and Weber 1985, cited in Stamp 1990:58).

Recently, development planners have been gaining a new appreciation of traditional technologies in water purification. For example, the United Nations Economic and Social Council noted that one of the reasons for the failure to meet the goals of the International Drinking Water and Sanitation Decade (1981 to 1990) was that the technologies applied were too sophisticated (Evans 1991). Shiva (1989:215) describes traditional methods employed by women in Africa and India to clarify and purify water using wood, seeds, and leaves from trees. Various trees have antibacterial and antifungal qualities that can be employed for this purpose, and some provide nutritious fruits as well (see INSTRAW 1991). Introducing appropriate technology in water projects (and other types of development projects) is a complex matter requiring detailed information for planners and a high level of community participation.

EXTENSION AND TRAINING

Women's interest in new irrigation and domestic water technology can be put to use by projects that recruit and train women for water management positions (Elmendorf and Isely 1983). A project in Bolivia trained women who were from 17 to 25 years old in the maintenance of water and sanitation facilities. Some of these Bolivian women later took full charge of the water facilities (Stein 1977, cited in Elmendorf 1980). Similarly, Cloud (1982) indicates that women in India, Sri Lanka, and the Philippines have successfully served as community organizers for women's water users' associations. In Maharastra state in India, women and men worked together to organize a lift irrigation scheme (Gram Gourav Pratistan Trust n.d., cited in Cloud 1982). In Sri Lanka and the Philippines, women served as government community water organizers (Uphoff 1981, 1982a, 1982b, cited in Cloud 1982). In India, women have been trained as hand-pump caretakers, who are responsible for maintaining the pumps and serving as liaisons between users at the village level and the authorities responsible for project implementation (Black 1990). When women are fully integrated into all aspects of project planning and project-affiliated water organizations, they are in a better position to ensure that they receive the full benefit of any water system improvements.

COMMUNITY PLANNING

Host-country training sessions, called Diagnostic Analysis Workshops, have proven useful in directing attention to women's water needs. Workshops are jointly led by donor and host-country experts, and participants are representatives of government ministries. Although earlier groups did not usually include women, the later inclusion of donor and host-country women has greatly strengthened these efforts. In the Sri Lanka Mahawelli Resettlement Scheme and the Madhya Pradesh Minor Irrigation Project in India, field teams collected extensive information on women's roles in water and farming systems and involved women in community water planning (Cloud 1984; Stanbury 1984). As a result, project input was directed toward host-country rural women, who were able to learn about the new water technology.

The goals of rural water projects usually include improving water delivery for crop irrigation and household use, and projects that bypass women at any stage from conception to completion risk failure because women are intimately involved in the procurement and use of water. This discussion of women and water illustrates the interconnected nature of water and development: new technologies for water delivery must be appropriate;

animal projects must include plans for water procurement; irrigation projects must include women or they may result in decreased rather than increased production; and forestry projects will flourish only if water is available for trees. The list could be extended. Water project planning must include all sectors of targeted communities, especially women, and must take into account the links between water management, agricultural production, health, and all aspects of the quality of life of rural people.

11

AGROFORESTRY

Judith Warner and Ellen Hansen

Forestry has often been considered a man's activity, an assumption which overlooks women's roles in Third World countries as collectors of fuelwood, users of tree products, and caretakers of forests (Dankelman and Davidson 1988; FAO 1991; Fortmann 1984; Hoskins 1979; Shiva 1989). In India, for example, women use wood for cooking and forest by-products for food and fodder. Women also collect honey, extract oil from seeds and nuts, and make wooden handicrafts for sale (Bhatty 1984). In keeping with their high level of involvement in forest harvesting and by-product use, they often work as wage laborers on plantation sites, digging holes and planting and watering trees. Third World women's roles in forestry are thus multiple and complex, and the inclusion of women as agroforestry project participants and beneficiaries is essential. Successful agroforestry projects will ensure access to land, capital, and resources for women as well as men and take into consideration the effects project inputs may have on women's time allocation for agricultural and household tasks (Fortmann 1985).

THE GENDER DIVISION OF LABOR

Before a project is designed, baseline research can indicate the gender division of labor in forestry activities. In particular, the responsibility of caring for trees should be determined before disseminating project inputs and extension information. Land tenure and tree tenure exist in a wide variety of forms in Third World countries, depending on tradition, economic conditions, and government policies (Bruce 1989; Fortmann and Bruce 1988; Hoskins 1979). Traditional gender divisions of labor are changing in the Third World as economic and environmental conditions change. Women are negatively affected by forestry projects that focus on single cash crops or commercial timber from trees, which are generally controlled by men (Dankelman and Davidson 1988) because women tend to concentrate on multi-use trees that provide food, fodder, fibers, and fuelwood (FAO 1990).

Women and men thus participate differently in forestry activities and have varying control over trees, land, and forest products. Women's food security strategies depend on a wide range of products harvested from trees on private land and in open public forests (FAO 1990). Women also traditionally collect water and fuelwood, transport, store and process food, and raise animals. As men migrate seasonally or permanently to work for wages, however, and as environmental conditions are altered, this traditional division of labor is changing (FAO/SIDA n.d.; Shiva 1989).

TIME ALLOCATION

A study in Nepal showed that as deforestation increased, firewood consumption decreased and total time for collection of fuelwood, leaf fodder, and grass increased by 1.13 hours per day for women in the most highly impacted area of the study (Kumar and Hotchkiss 1988:9). The authors point out that as more of women's time is consumed by longer trips to wooded areas, they have less time to devote to agricultural production, resulting in lowered household consumption of food and decreased nutritional status. Reduced availability of fodder for animals means livestock must forage and graze, which increases pressure on local land. This example is cited to reinforce the links between various aspects of people's lives and health and issues that include the allocation of scarce resources, such as time.

Women face two types of labor constraints relative to agroforestry activities: (1) women, especially those who head households, may not have sufficient time to devote to caring for trees, and (2) the time and labor requirements of agroforestry activities compete with other demands on women's time, resulting in increased work for them (Fortmann 1985). Trees necessitate care, harvesting, and by-product processing. The time required for labor at each of these stages is a critical aspect of any potential project. For example, Fortmann (1985) points out that schemes involving cut-and-carry fodder trees can create additional work for women, who are often required to do the tree planting. Failure to consider the time and labor constraints women face can result in project failure.

Careful scheduling is necessary to avoid time conflicts between agricultural and agroforestry labor demands. Hoskins (1979) suggests that seed collection and nursery or soil preparation should be scheduled before peak agricultural seasons. She cites the case of a palm oil project in which planners and men's cooperative members did not take into account that women had limited time during the harvest season to process palm oil. As a result, most of the palm fruit spoiled.

Agroforestry projects can incorporate some successful labor-saving features. Inter-row planting of trees and crops is useful because it eliminates weeding a separate crop. Another technique for modifying women's labor requirements is alley farming, which involves growing food crops within alleys formed of leguminous hedgerows and which provides for soil regeneration, fertilizer, livestock fodder, fuel, and food (Cashman 1986). Alley farming is a compact, multipurpose system that can result in time saved in fuelwood collecting as trees mature and provide nearby sources of wood.

Fuel

Many Third World countries depend almost entirely on firewood and crop residues for their energy needs, a situation that is likely to continue in future decades. This dependency has contributed to deforestation (Dankelman and Davidson 1988; French 1978; Haile 1989). Whether on a large or small scale, deforestation imposes heavy burdens on rural women, the traditional gatherers of firewood, by requiring more travel time to cover greater distances, and participation of more women and girls to gather the fuel. When distances to fuel sources become too great, women may have to purchase wood from men who own carts (French 1978). Women who gather and sell fuelwood to support their families are also affected, because they devote larger portions of each day to traveling to their source areas (Haile 1989). When crop residues and dung are used either as replacements for or additions to firewood, deforestation has additional negative impacts on women's crop and animal production tasks. Such practices lead to reduced soil fertility, loss of agricultural output, and reduced animal fodder (Dankelman and Davidson 1988).

As fuelwood sources are depleted, especially near large cities, many women have become involved in the commercialization of forest products as fuel. Female fuelwood carriers in Ethiopia, for example, spend as much as seven hours a day gathering and transporting forest products for sale, an estimate that increases as nearby supplies are diminished (Haile 1989).

Women are often willing to experiment with new ways of using other fuel sources, such as plant stalks, dung, and charcoal (Hoskins 1979) and with new types of stoves (FAO/SIDA n.d.). Residents in areas of increasing fuel shortages are changing their cooking and eating practices and turning to foods with shorter cooking time when they can. Often, however, people simply eat fewer cooked meals per day. If edible raw nutritional foods are not available, the quality of their diet declines.

Important factors in project planning include the current role of women in the acquisition, utilization, and management of fuel resources (especially wood, crop residues, and dung) and women's other agriculturally related activities, which affect their access to fuel resources and the time available to exploit these resources. It is important that development practitioners compile an adequate data base describing the role of women in the management of domestic fuel resources and integrate it with an assessment of appropriate technologies for more efficient fuel use. To be considered appropriate, these technologies need to be based on and compatible with local social and environmental conditions, especially women's time constraints.

Animal Forage

The world fuel shortage has adversely affected the availability of forest leaves and fruits and has created problems for women who collect forest products for the small ruminants they own. As local sources of animal forage are exhausted, women spend increasing amounts of time searching for fodder for their animals. Alternatively, women may lose control of animal products for their daily household needs and be forced to entrust their animals to male herders, who can travel greater distances with larger herds in search of pasturage (Jain 1991).

ACCESS TO LAND

The factors that limit women's participation in forestry projects include competition for land and for space for tree planting (Hoskins 1979). Land competition occurs when agricultural cropping or other land uses compete with forests that supply fuelwood. Land use changes often restrict access to sites that formerly served as the source of forest products. The concentration of landownership has displaced many women in Third World countries; indeed, women have title to only 1 percent of the world's land, while worldwide they produce more than half its food (Dankelman and Davidson 1988).

Tree ownership is frequently used to establish permanent land rights (Fortmann 1985; Rocheleau 1988). For this reason, local traditions may exclude women from planting trees at all. In Tanzania a village land committee was willing to allocate land to women to grow beans but not coffee, a more profitable, but permanent, crop. In areas where women borrow or rent land, agroforestry projects for women may not be practical unless new use-right patterns are developed.

The degree to which women retain long-term control over trees has implications for the tree varieties they select. Women who have access to trees and tree products through their husbands and who farm their husband's land or live in a society characterized by marital instability may not be motivated to plant trees unless they are fast-maturing varieties whose products will be available relatively soon after planting (Fortmann 1985). Agroforestry projects can focus on lands to which women already have use rights or can include provisions for women's plots. In Nigeria, alley farming has reduced women's need for additional scarce land and has helped to establish their claim to lands they currently farm (Owusu-Bempah 1986).

Obtaining title to land can create problems for women, who have often been overlooked by government and project personnel and have seldom been given tenure on the lands they farm. Hoskins (1979) indicates that women often lack the political leverage to request and maintain land tenure, and Noronha and Lethem (1983, cited in Bruce 1989) note that legal land tenure and actual practice are often very different. Examples from Haiti and Syria indicate that although laws exist to ensure equal inheritance by women and men, women in fact lose access to land in favor of brothers or even tenants or sharecroppers. Kenya and Ghana have recently passed laws granting land and other rights to women (Manuh 1989), but laws by themselves will not change social relations or attitudes or eradicate gender-based inequalities. Laws allocating land to men with the assumption that men will share equally with women may result in further restrictions of women's access to land for forestry (FAO/SIDA n.d.).

Recognition from local, regional, and national governments of women's roles in forestry is important in establishing women's secure legal access to land. Involving women in development projects as decision makers, acknowledging their roles as heads of households, and including them in project planning and implementation are all elements of a process of improving women's access to land (Bruce 1989; Manuh 1989). Project planners need to investigate women's forestry land needs and work with women to establish long-term land-use rights, or women's access to land may be further restricted.

TREE SELECTION

Firewood burns at different speeds and levels of heat intensity, and the wrong type of wood can set roofs afire or impart a disagreeable taste to food (FAO/SIDA n.d.; Fortmann 1985; Hoskins 1982). In addition, fuelwood is used for other purposes besides cooking. It is necessary, for example, to provide fires for silk making, salt making, keeping insects away from people and animals, keeping people and their animals warm, and for ritual purposes (FAO/SIDA n.d.). Beyond using trees for fuelwood, women and men harvest fruit, sap, and flowers from trees for food; leaves for fodder; many parts of trees for medicines, dyes, and fibers; branches for fences and household implements; and trunks for furniture and boats (Bruce 1989; Dankelman and Davidson 1988; FAO/SIDA n.d.; Feldstein and Poats 1989; Shiva 1989). Certain varieties of trees serve to fix soil and promote soil and water conservation. Some serve as living fences. Others add organic matter as fertilizer and fix nitrogen in the soil. Thus the full range of people's wood product needs must be explored when introducing new varieties of trees or culling trees from local areas. For example, women beer brewers require large quantities of fuelwood and therefore might be willing to participate in a women's cooperative woodlot to serve their needs (Fortmann 1985).

To promote the acceptance of agroforestry projects, Owusu-Bempah (1986) suggests selecting tree species that meet family nutritional, fuel, and health needs. Her research in Ghana showed that women can provide useful information for selecting trees and are better at tree conservation than men. In a survey by the Food and Agriculture Organization of the United Nations (FAO) in Sierra Leone, women knew and gathered 31 products from the nearby forest, while men knew only 8 (FAO/SIDA n.d.). Current forestry and farming practices are vital elements of development project design. Working with women, project planners can take into account the various needs met by different types of trees when selecting trees for planting.

CONTROL OVER RESOURCES

Women invest time and labor in utilizing and establishing control over forest resources. Forestry development projects have failed in the past because they did not consider women's needs or interests. In Niger, for example, women were uninterested in participating in a forestry project except in the case of the baobab tree, where women maintained individual rights to the fruit (Barrès et al. 1975). In the Indian village of Gadkharkh, women stand guard around community forest lands to protect the trees from illegal cutting. They also established a seedling nursery to produce the types of trees they find most useful. "Each sapling in the Gadkharkh plantations is nurtured with great care and tenderness by people who have control over the product" (Dankelman and Davidson 1988:60). An FAO study in Dominica showed that while women had control of tree products near the homestead, farther away men controlled the products even when women provided labor and had the responsibility for caring for the trees (FAO 1991).

The Chipko movement of the Himalayan foothills in India began because of conflicts over the exploitation of forests. The deforestation of steep slopes by commercial loggers (operating with government permits) and in some areas by poor local land-management practices resulted in heavy erosion and destruction of the homes and sources of livelihood of village residents. Chipko began as a male organization, but once involved, women quickly became active and in some areas dominant in organizing protests. Chipko is a Hindi word that means "hugging" and that describes the women's method of protest: by hugging the trees, they faced down the loggers—and in some cases the men in their villages—who wished to cut down trees vital to the women's survival. An interesting aspect of women's involvement in the Chipko movement is that the women are demanding a change in gender relations; that is, they are claiming the right to share with men in decision making while at the same time resisting change in the form of development, logging, and other activities that threaten their lives (Jain 1991).

Kenya's Green Belt Movement is a very successful program that is based on grassroots participation and that involves women at all levels. Members of the movement, mostly women, have established more than 600 tree nurseries and have planted 7 million trees (Maathai 1988:25). Many factors have contributed to the success of the Green Belt Movement. For example, many of the members of the movement are employed in its nurseries or as advisors or promoters; the movement has encouraged the use of indigenous species; it has involved communities, including schoolchildren, in its activities; and it remains flexible and is committed to reforestation in Kenyan communities. Maathai (1988:31) notes that while the movement was "conceived by and is directed by women, both men and children have enthusiastically participated."

A different project in Kenya, however, presents an alternative outcome: when women were not guaranteed benefits from their labor in watering seedlings in a nursery run by men, their other daily activities took precedence over hauling water for seedlings during drought conditions. This conflict points out the need to ensure that women as well as men will benefit from the labor they dedicate to the project (Raintree 1987). Bhatty (1984) asserts that government and community nursery projects are suitable for women's participation and further that project planners must be careful that such projects do not exclude women from leadership roles.

Laws sometimes protect and ensure women's access to and control over trees and forest products, but women often depend on family or marital status for such rights (Rocheleau 1988). Indeed, recent laws have sometimes changed traditional systems of ownership of resources and have resulted in a loss of control of land and trees for women (Chavangi, Engelhard and Jones 1988; Shiva 1989). To enhance women's access to and control of those products that are necessary to their lives, changes in legal codes must be based on accurate information about existing rights, or lack of them, concerning tenure and control.

Complementarity of men's and women's roles in forestry can reinforce use rights. Women generally harvest different tree products, such as fuelwood and food, than do men, who may be interested in timber and other commercial products (FAO 1991). A project in Tanzania resulted in women's access to common land for fuelwood lots in spite of men's traditional control of communal land and tree planting. Project planners approached the issue by discussing improved stoves, which they hoped would partially mitigate the problem of decreased fuelwood supplies. Male village authorities agreed that women's fuelwood lots located on common land would help resolve fuel problems and supported the women's plan to plant trees and maintain the lots. The project was seen as a means of increasing cooking efficiency and augmenting fuelwood supply and was therefore not perceived as a threat to grazing activities on the common land (FTPP 1989).

INCOME GENERATION

Women throughout the world collect tree products for household use and occasional sale, and these activities could be intensified to increase their income-generating potential. Especially for very poor rural women, sales of firewood and charcoal are an important source of livelihood (FAO

1990; Haile 1989; Hoskins 1979). Women who have access to common forest lands are able to exploit forest products for income generation with little or no initial investment and with flexibility of work time and season. Women who have few other sources of income use forest fibers to make mats and baskets for sale and sell herbs and remedies.

Landless women in India are extensively involved in the production of beedi—small cigarettes rolled in leaves harvested from local forests. A report by the FAO (1991:75) estimates that millions of women in Asia participate in harvesting the leaves and rolling the beedi at the level of the individual or small enterprise—2.5 million people in India alone. Beedi production and leaf harvesting are important sources of income for landless women with few other options for employment.

Women's work is important in reforestation programs. In Indonesia women are involved in preparing nursery beds, broadcasting tree seeds, transplanting, and maintaining nurseries, including fertilizing, spraying for plant pests, and setting out young plants (Hartono 1984). In Senegal, women undertook tree planting to preserve local soil fertility and to provide fuel. When a seedling shortage occurred, local women's groups initiated profitable backyard nurseries to supply seedlings. Female extension agents' introduction of appropriate technology facilitated this effort (Hoskins 1979). Paolisso and Yudelman (1991:18) note that, in parts of Latin America, work in nurseries is "one of the most common and culturally accepted roles for women in reforestation," partly because the nurseries tend to be located near water sources or within the community, allowing women to tend seedlings at the same time that they take care of their other obligations.

Hoskins (1979) suggests that community reforestation projects that benefit the local environment should pay individuals for tree planting and care. Whether participants should gain income from forestry development projects is a question planners must answer early in project design because paying for services rendered by participants can create problems. For example, if local caretakers believe that the project will own the crop, they may not feel personally responsible for tree care. Spears noted that herders in Niger pulled up trees that had been planted as part of a World Bank project on traditional grazing land without consulting them (Spears 1978, cited in Dankelman and Davidson 1988). Without the interest and cooperation of local residents, forestry projects may therefore not only fail but may raise the ire of local people and damage possibilities for future forestry projects.

Capital

Whether project planners should charge for seedlings is another a major issue in project design. Trees given free of charge to project participants may not be well cared for, but if a charge is instituted, many women, especially those who head households, may not be able to afford them. An incentive payment based on tree survival rates can offset this effect.

Wage Labor

The types of positions and wage levels at which women are employed in forestry industries varies. Dankelman and Davidson (1988) note that, while women in Kenya have played a major role in tree planting, they are generally relegated to low-paying, menial positions when they find wage labor in forestry. In Malaysia, many women workers are employed in veneer and plywood mills as machine operators or manual workers but are paid lower wages than men because most are in so-called unskilled positions. Men tend to be employed in administrative, clerical, sales, and service positions, which pay higher wages. Similarly, in Thailand, where 20 percent of all forest workers are women, women are more likely than men to be employed in nursery and plantation work due to their lower prevailing wage rate (FAO 1984b). In contrast, female laborers in reforestation programs in the Philippines were paid at the same wage rate as men and were judged highly efficient. Women were also hired as finishers in plywood manufacturing and as research technicians in wood-based industries (Cruz 1984).

When men who lack gender consciousness are in decision- and policy-making positions, women's needs are often overlooked. In Kenya, extension work is considered suitable for women, although few women have received the technical training necessary to become extension agents (Dankelman and Davidson 1988). The FAO recommends that women be targeted for training programs and recruited as supervisory staff in government ministries in order to increase the number of women professionals in forestry (FAO 1990).

APPROPRIATE TECHNOLOGY

Many forestry projects attempt to introduce fuel-saving appropriate technology to help conserve forestry resources. Women who have been responsible for household cooking and for meeting fuel needs have many traditional strategies for carrying out those activities. Such strategies should be taken into account before new technologies are designed. The three-stone stove or other traditional stoves, for example, may prove to be more energy efficient, if properly managed, than new stoves. Depending on local circumstances and availability, the use of traditional fuels such as dung should not necessarily be discouraged in favor of newer, more expensive fuels. Instead, making more efficient use of readily available fuels could prove more productive. In selecting a stove, women may consider health, convenience, and other factors more important than fuel savings alone (Stamp 1990).

New village-based technologies that use solar energy, wind, flowing water, or organic farm wastes are being introduced in Third World countries. Before substantial investments in new technologies are made, however, women's activity patterns and the technologies' possible impact on forest resources need to be investigated. Solar stoves, for example, are not necessarily useful or successful in societies in which women cook mostly after the sun is down or where the stoves require changes in cooking patterns that are inconsistent with local utensils, foods, or cooking methods (Stamp 1990). When women are involved in the design, construction, and installation of alternative stoves appropriate to their particular needs, stove projects are more likely to succeed (Dankelman and Davidson 1988). Therefore, while solar cookers have great potential to reduce the need for fuelwood, their success is not guaranteed in all areas.

One successful effort to introduce appropriate forestry technologies is the Renewable Energy Technology Project, in Lesotho (Davenport 1984). From the beginning, the project indicated a high level of gender awareness and targeted women as participants. Throughout the project, women were repeatedly consulted about the design of household cooking, heating, and insulation technologies. Technicians made modifications based on women's opinions, and many of the extension agents who later introduced the technologies were women. Consequently, women's household labor was made easier, safer, and more convenient and efficient. The new cookstoves cut fuel use, thereby reducing the time necessary for fuel collecting.

Appropriate Technology and Tree Preservation

When designing forestry projects that combine appropriate technology with tree preservation, attention should be given to villagers' perceptions of the scarcity of existing resources. Problems related to fuel shortages may be viewed as secondary when compared to those of a lack of arable land or

forage. In Burundi, where the use of trees for local fuelwood was drain-
ing resources, a project was implemented to protect the Burundi Forest
(Davenport 1984). The project proposed to develop plantations around the
forest, set up seedling nurseries, and foster private and community woodlots. Inexpensive fuel-saving stoves were introduced as well. Women were
expected to benefit from project activities through increased fuelwood
supplies and improved cookstoves, so women's opinions were solicited regarding project activities, particularly with regard to cookstove design.

One potential problem with the Burundi Forest project is planners' assumptions that cookstoves will save fuelwood and that these savings will
reduce pressure on the forest (Davenport 1984). These assumptions may
not hold true. Cookstoves, when utilized in the field, may not prove as efficient as when tested in the laboratory. Some stoves require continued
gathering of wood to produce charcoal (Stamp 1990). Fuel collection is often a minor pressure on forest resources when compared to grazing, agriculture, and lumbering (Dankelman and Davidson 1988; Haile 1989; World
Bank 1990).

EXTENSION SERVICES

Recruitment of Women Foresters

Although forestry has been considered an inappropriate profession for
women in the past, women are becoming increasingly involved in the
field. In India, women foresters facilitate communication with local
women when cultural tradition hinders free contact between women and
men. Bhatty (1984) suggests that the many educated women could attend
forestry schools and return home to work with their mothers and neighbors. In the Philippines, university programs have begun graduating large
numbers of women foresters and forest rangers and seem to be overcom-
ing traditional gender biases (Cruz 1984).

In contrast, in Indonesia the number of educated and rural women involved in forestry is low because of the belief that women may not have
sufficient stamina for the work and would need protection against wild
animals and strangers in distant forest areas (Hartono 1984). A similar situation exists in Thailand, where most women forest service personnel work
in office or research positions, and in Kenya, where more women work
as agriculture and community development extension workers than as forestry extensionists (Feldstein, Rocheleau, and Buck 1989). Dankelman and
Davidson (1988) point out that the lack of women at the extension level

and in policy-making positions is partly a result of social factors. For example, boys have more educational opportunities than girls, and forestry is generally regarded as men's work, too dangerous and difficult for women. A 1985 FAO report emphasizes that women and men forestry workers and others responsible for implementing forestry programs need adequate incentives for staying in the profession.

Extension Services for Women

Agroforestry extension personnel must contact women in order to collect information on women's involvement in forestry activities, gather information about the local environment, and provide training on local forestry concerns (Fortmann 1985). Women's knowledge of forests and forest products can be vital to the success of any forestry project. In their discussion of a case study from western Kenya, Feldstein, Rocheleau, and Buck (1989) develop the idea of extension work that includes local people as knowledgeable practitioners of forestry activities. They stress the need for techniques that ensure that women's voices are heard as well as men's and that local women and men are involved in the design, planning, and implementation of projects.

Madhya Pradesh Social Forestry, a successful project, has sought to teach communal and private forest management and production skills by setting up a forestry extension organization, distributing seedlings, and establishing communal plantations. Throughout the project, women's needs and gender issues have been taken into account. Despite problems in finding qualified women for positions as foresters, women have been integrated into the project at all levels. Where women extension agents have worked, village women have supported project activities, while in areas with no female agents women's levels of awareness and support have been lower (Davenport 1984).

COMMUNITY PLANNING

Community forestry projects require local participants to set forestry priorities. Unfortunately, women have often been underrepresented in discussions with community leaders and village councils. As a result, tree projects have failed when women's role in the division of labor was overlooked. For example, projects may distribute trees to men in a society in which women have traditionally cared for the trees. If women have little time, lack an understanding of project benefits, or do not share in the benefits, the trees will die (Hoskins 1979).

The "top down" approach to forestry is not effective. A Sierra Leone project that sought to establish fuel-producing woodlots on garden plots close to the village met resistance from village women (Hoskins 1984). Because garden land was scarce and fuel was available, women could not see the need for the proposed woodlots. They preferred planting selected species around garden edges or on fallow plots. Project planners must determine the local acceptability of project inputs before initiating activities so that women's true needs are met.

In a case from Honduras, the Honduran Forestry Development Corporation (COHDAFOR) involved communities in terrace construction and reforestation (Wiff 1984). Although this project had not targeted women, women were more interested and more accepting of new ideas than were men, and women's success with project activities led to increased community participation.

Because male informants may take women's forestry contributions for granted, project planners have not always noticed women's activities (Hoskins 1979). Men often do not know what women know or do. Stamp (1990:154) cites a 1956 study by Lambert in which men said they did not know why women called gatherings, whether it was for casual interaction or specific purposes. To overcome this type of communication problem, community forestry projects should be based on, or should at least include, women's knowledge. Local women should be interviewed about their work cycles and their forest by-product needs. Fortmann (1985) recommends the Diagnosis and Design approach developed by the International Council for Research in Agro-Forestry (ICRAF 1983). This method involves detailed interviews with local women and men about their needs, production system activities, and constraints in implementing agroforestry activities. Raintree's manual for diagnosis and design assumes that women have a role in the process as field extension workers and as farmers (Raintree 1987:36–48).

Forests play a vital role in the lives of rural agricultural people. As many areas of the Third World are experiencing deforestation at alarming rates, women's efforts to maintain their families become more complicated. Loss of forests means women spend more time collecting forest products essential to their lives, which limits time remaining for other, also essential, tasks, including subsistence and cash agricultural production. Deforestation results in soil degradation, which also has an impact on women's and men's abilities to provide food and on their access to clean water. The interconnected nature of these issues has been increasingly recognized, yet women remain peripheral in the minds of many development agencies and planners. Cultural and institutional barriers to women's full participation in development projects in forestry and other areas remain in place, although some case studies cited in this chapter indicate that change is taking place. To facilitate further change, continued research is necessary on women's skills and knowledge of agroforestry and on constraints to women's forestry activities. Involving women in the planning, design, and implementation of forestry projects should be a vital factor in any national or international development program. Support for women's efforts, such as in the Chipko movement in India and the Kenyan Green Belt Movement, should be incorporated into national development policy. Trees and forests play a critical role in the health of people and the environment, and women as users, managers, and protectors of forests have much to offer their communities.

CONCLUSION

Helen Kreider Henderson

The primary goal of this book is to acknowledge and make available to a wide community a corpus of valuable information on gender issues in agricultural development collected over more than twenty-five years. The book presents various analytical approaches to gender issues in agriculture and indicates further resources for obtaining appropriate data.

The primary sources for the material presented here are observations about farm women's lives and work as recorded by researchers and development personnel. Design or evaluation surveys, funded through international development agencies, have often provided the primary setting, but equally important studies have been initiated within Third World countries themselves. The way in which this research has exposed the effects on women of their differential access to such resources as land, income, credit, technology, and extension services constitutes a major theme.

After being largely ignored during the colonial era, gender and development issues became prominent in the early 1970s as governments and nongovernmental agencies increasingly began to link improvements in the standard of living of people in the Third World with recognition of the importance of women's role in agriculture.

Formerly, agricultural experts often assumed that women's farming, marketing, and household work was part of a system of "traditional" and "balanced" sex roles, needing little further consideration. What was not seen was how changes in agricultural systems have frequently redirected labor from subsistence or previously established cash cropping and have affected the labor patterns of women, often increasing women's work in areas of subsistence cropping, cash cropping, and food processing.

Influenced by the concepts and methods of gender analysis, development practitioners and researchers have developed new approaches to data collection concerning changes in farming systems, which identified women as workers and considered both field work and household work as productive work. An assessment of the varieties of households, including the growing phenomenon of women-headed households and the recognition that even within a household there may be several economic decision makers, became more important in such research projects.

Worldwide, time allocation studies have shown how women's work is distributed and how workloads in farming, marketing, and housework mutually influence one another. Because of such studies, we can now see that farm women generally had less time for relaxation than did male farmers and less time for attending public meetings and promoting political agendas (McSweeney 1979a). Other studies exposed the effects on women of differential access to resources—land, time, income, credit, technology, and extension services—and the increasing demands on women resulting from male out-migration.

Research on gender issues deriving from farmers' local knowledge and perspectives was presented to largely resistant audiences of development planners and decision makers (who were overwhelmingly male). The research findings, however, were presented in such a way as to substantiate the critical importance of women's contributions to the rural economy, and they set the stage for policy-changing arguments that aimed to protect and improve women's access to and control of economic resources as well as their right to participate in and benefit from increased economic opportunities in their communities. Presented in training programs for donor agency personnel over many years, the message has had some impact, at least in identifying "practical gender needs" of women farmers in specific contexts (Molyneaux 1985:233). Third World women's organizations have themselves begun framing a variety of "strategic" arguments for women's empowerment.

The number and diversity of references in this book point to the breadth and depth of the research that has now been accomplished, and the wide span of project experience shows both past mistakes and successes. Although there is much regional diversity, the data also indicate many commonalities in how women's stake in development is often undermined. While Western women predominate in the earlier works cited here, Third World researchers are increasingly defining what is important for study and action, and the bibliography reflects their contributions. This growing

involvement indicates the increased organizational strength of these researchers and the recognition of the importance of their perspectives by
planners and scholars from the First and Third Worlds. Community spokes-
persons and women's groups throughout the Third World are also insist-
ing on recognition of their points of view. They are initiating agricultural
agendas and making demands for the legal recognition of women's stake in
development resources (Bunch and Carrillo 1991).

The text directs the reader to see women as active decision makers and
organizers in social, economic, and political contexts. We argue that recognizing women as prime agricultural actors and acknowledging their intel-
lectual and physical contributions is a critical step toward implementing
appropriate action in development planning on the local, national, and
international level.

Projects that involve both women and men in needs assessment, design,
management, and benefits can bring increased skills and services to all
members of the community. The choices for action on poverty are not
simple. Understanding diversity and learning from the past should lead development planners and local community organizers to ask more directly
about gender relations and to require detailed community involvement at
all phases of project development. It is our hope that the research referred
to here will be debated, reinterpreted, and built on for more equitable and
sustainable development for both women and men.

REFERENCES

ABBREVIATIONS

UNSAID	United States Agency for International Development
CAM	Centro Acción de las Mujeres
CEPAL	Comisión Económica Para América Latina
FA—CIPRES	Fundación Arias para la Paz y el Progreso Humano-Centro para la Investigación y la Promoción del Desarrollo Rural y Social (Arias Foundation for Peace and Human Progress—Center for Research and Promotion of Rural and Social Development)
FAO	Food and Agriculture Organization of the United Nations
FAO/SIDA	FAO and the Swedish International Development Agency
FTPP	Forests, Trees and People Programme
ICRAF	International Council for Research in Agro-Forestry
INSTRAW	United Nations International Research and Training Institute for the Advancement of Women
ICRW	International Center for Research on Women
ISIS	Women's International Information and Communication Service
UNDP	United Nations Development Program
UNHCR	United Nations High Commissioner for Refugees

Abreu, Luz Maria. 1989. The Experience of MUDE Dominicana in Operating a Women-Specific Credit Program. In Berger and Buvinic 1989, 161–73.

Acharya, Meena, and Lynn Bennett. 1981. *The Rural Women of Nepal: An Aggregate Analysis and Summary of Eight Village Studies.* Kathmandu, Nepal: Centre for Economic Development and Administration.

———. 1983. *Women and the Subsistence Sector: Economic Participation and Household Decisionmaking in Nepal.* Washington, D.C.: World Bank.

Adams, Patricia, and Lawrence Solomon. 1991. *In The Name of Progress: The Underside of Foreign Aid.* Toronto: Energy Probe Research Foundation.

Adepoju, Aderanti. 1994. The Demographic Profile: Sustained High Mortality and Fertility and Migration for Employment. In Adepoju and Oppong 1994, 17–34.

Adepoju, Aderanti, and Christine Oppong, eds. 1994. *Gender, Work and Population in Sub-Saharan Africa.* London: James Currey, for the International Labour Office.

Agarwal, Bina. 1987. Gender Issues in the Agricultural Modernization of India. In Momsen and Townsend 1987, 334–36.

———. 1988. Neither Sustenance Nor Sustainability: Agricultural Strategies, Ecological Degradation and Indian Women in Poverty. In *Structures of Patriarchy: State, Community and Household in Modernizing Asia,* 83–130. London: Zed.

———. 1992a. Cold Hearths and Barren Slopes: The Woodfuel Crisis in the Third World. In *Inventing Women: Science, Technology and Gender,* ed. Gill Kirkup and Laurie Smith Keller, 255–65. Cambridge: Polity Press.

———. 1992b. Gender Relations and Food Security: Coping with Seasonality, Drought, and Famine in South Asia. In Benería and Feldman 1992, 181–218.

Ahmed, Iftikhar. 1985. Conclusion. In *Technology and Rural Women: Conceptual and Empirical Issues,* ed. Iftikhar Ahmed, 327–41. London: George Allen and Unwin.

Ahmed-Ghosh, Huma. 1993. Agricultural Development and Work Pattern of Women in a North Indian Village. In Raju and Bagchi 1993, 180–95.

Akeroyd, Anne V. 1991. Gender, Food Production and Property Rights: Constraints on Women Farmers in Southern Africa. In *Women, Development and Survival in the Third World,* ed. Haleh Afshar, 139–71. London: Longman.

Alvarez, Sonia E. 1990. *Engendering Democracy in Brazil: Women's Movements in Transition Politics.* Princeton, N.J.: Princeton University Press.

Anderson, Cecilia. 1992. Practical Guidelines. In Ostergaard 1992, 165–97.

Anderson, Mary. 1985. Technology Transfer: Implications for Women. In Overholt et al. 1985, 57–78.

Anker, Richard. 1983. Effect on Reported Levels of Female Labor Force Participation in Developing Countries of Questionnaire Design, Sex of Interviewer and Self/Proxy Status of Respondent: Description of a Methodological Field Experiment. World Employment Research Programme Research Working Paper (restricted). Geneva: International Labour Office. Mimeographed.

———. 1994. Measuring Women's Participation in the African Labour Force. In Adepoju and Oppong 1994, 64–75.

Anker, R., M. E. Khan, and R. B. Gupta. 1987. Biases in Measuring the Labour Force: Results of a Methods Test Survey in Uttar Pradesh, India. *International Labour Review,* 126 (2):151–67.

Antrobus, Peggy. 1992. Women and the Informal Sector: Priorities for Socially Sustainable Development. *Development* 3:54–56.

Appropriate Technology. 1991. Benefits All Round for Women Stove Producers in Western Kenya. *Appropriate Technology* 18 (3): Insert.

Arias, Maria Eugenia. 1989. The Rural Development Fund: An Integrated Credit Program for Small and Medium Entrepreneurs. In Berger and Buvinic 1989, 201–13.

Arizpe, Lourdes, and Josefina Aranda. 1981. The "Comparative Advantages" of Women's Disadvantages: Women Workers in the Strawberry Export Agribusiness in Mexico. *Signs* 7 (2): 453–73.

Arizpe, Lourdes, and Carlota Botey. 1987. Mexican Agricultural Development Policy and Its Impact on Rural Women. In Deere and Leon 1987, 67–83.

Badri, Balghis. 1986. Women, Land Ownership and Development in the Sudan. *Canadian Woman Studies* 7:89–92.

Bagchi, Deipica. 1993. The Household and Extrahousehold Work of Rural Women in a Changing Resource Environment in Madhya Pradesh, India. In Raju and Bagchi 1993, 137–57.

Bardhan, Kalpana. 1993. Work in South Asia: An Inter-regional Perspective. In Raju and Bagchi 1993, 39–73.

Barnes, Virginia. 1984. *Changes in Crop Mixtures and Their Relationship to Gender Role Changes Among the Lugbara.* WID Working Paper No. 2. Women and International Development, Joint Harvard/MIT Group. Cambridge, Mass.: Harvard Institute for International Development.

Baroin, Catherine. 1987. The Position of Tubu Women in Pastoral Production: Daza Kesherda, Republic of Niger. *Ethnos* 52 (1–2):137–55.

Barrès, Vicky, Piera Brigata, Annette Corrée, Madeleine Debourg, Marie-Jo Doucet, Véronique Gentil, Sylvia Malachowski, Franca Pieressa, and Odette Snoy. 1975. *La participation des femmes rurales au développement: A Propos d'une action d'animation rurale féminine en Republique de Niger, 1966–67.* Paris: Institut de Recherches et d'Applications des Methods de Développement (IRAM).

Barrow, Christine. 1993. Small Farm Food Production and Gender in Barbados. In Momsen 1993b, 181–93.

Basson, Priscilla. 1981. Women and Traditional Food Technologies: Changes in Rural Jordan. *Ecology of Food and Nutrition* 2:17–23.

Bay, Edna, ed. 1982. *Women and Work in Africa.* Boulder, Colo.: Westview Press.

Begum, Kohinoor. 1989. Participation of Rural Women in Income-Earning Activities: A Case Study of a Bangladesh Village. *Women's Studies International Forum* 12 (5): 519–28.

Bekele, Fetenu. 1982. Report of Mission to DANA and Golgotta Settlement Schemes. Addis Ababa, Ethiopia. Mimeographed.

Benería, Lourdes, and Shelley Feldman. 1992. *Unequal Burden: Economic Crises, Persistent Poverty, and Women's Work.* Boulder, Colo.: Westview Press.

Benería, Lourdes, and Martha Roldán. 1987. *The Crossroads of Class and Gender: Industrial Homework, Subcontracting, and Household Dynamics in Mexico City.* Chicago: University of Chicago Press.

Bennett, Lynn. 1983. *Preliminary Analytical Framework for Proposed Study on the Role of Women in Income Production and Intrahousehold Allocation of Resources as a Determinant of Child Health and Nutrition.* Geneva: WHO/UNICEF Seminar on the Determinants of Infant Feeding Practices.

Benson, Janet E., and Jan Paul Emmert. 1985. *The Accelerated Mahaweli Program, Sri Lanka: A Women in Development Assessment.* Washington, D.C.: USAID, Office of Women in Development.

Benton, Jane. 1987. A Decade of Change in the Lake Titicaca Region. In Momsen and Townsend 1987, 215–21.

———. 1993. The Role of Women's Organizations and Groups in Community Development: A Case Study of Bolivia. In *Different Places, Different Voices: Gender and Development in Africa, Asia and Latin America,* ed. Janet Momsen and Vivian Kinnaird, 230–42. International Studies of Women and Places Series. London: Routledge.

Berger, Marguerite. 1985. *Women's Access to Credit in the Informal Sector: Some Evidence from Ecuador and Peru.* WID Working Paper No. 5. WID Joint Harvard/MIT Group. Cambridge, Mass.: Harvard Institute for International Development.

———. 1989. Introduction. In Berger and Buvinic 1989, 1–18.

Berger, Marguerite, and Myra Buvinic, eds. 1988. *The Informal Sector, Microenterprise and Women's Work in Latin America.* Washington, D.C.: International Center for Research on Women.

———. 1989. *Women's Ventures: Assistance to the Informal Sector in Latin America.* West Hartford, Conn.: Kumarian Press.

Berger, M., V. Delancey, and A. Mellencamp. 1984. *Bridging the Gender Gap in Agricultural Extension.* Washington, D.C.: International Center for Research on Women.

Berleant-Schiller, Riva, and William M. Maurer. 1993. Women's Place Is Every Place: Merging Domains and Women's Roles in Barbuda and Dominica. In Momsen 1993b, 65–79.

Bernal, Victoria. 1988. Losing Ground: Women and Agriculture on Sudan's Irrigated Schemes; Lessons from a Blue Nile Village. In Davison 1988a, 131–56.

Besson, Jean. 1993. Reputation and Respectability Reconsidered: A New Perspective on Afro-Caribbean Peasant Women. In Momsen 1993b, 15–37.

Besteman, Catherine. 1989. Economic Strategies of Farming Households in Penabranca, Portugal. *Economic Development and Cultural Change* 38 (1): 129–43.

———. 1991. Land Tenure, Social Power, and the Legacy of Slavery in Southern Somalia. Ph.D. diss., University of Arizona.

Bhatty, Zarina. 1984. *Women in Forestry: India.* Rome: UN, FAO, Tigerpapers.

Bindocci, Cynthia Gay. 1993. *Women and Technology: An Annotated Bibliography.* New York: Garland Publishing.

Bisilliat, Jeanne, and Michele Fieloux. 1987. *Women of the Third World: Work and Daily Life.* London: Associated University Presses.

Black, Maggie. 1990. *From Handpumps to Health: The Evolution of Water and Sanitation Programmes in Bangladesh, India and Nigeria.* New York: United Nations Children's Fund.

Bleiburg, Fanny M., A. Brun Thierry, S. Goihman, and Emile Gouba. 1980. Duration of Activities and Energy Expenditure of Female Farmers in Dry and Rainy Seasons in Upper Volta. *British Journal of Nutrition* 43 (no. 71): 71–82.

Blumberg, Rae Lesser. 1981. Females, Farming and Food: Rural Development and Women's Participation in Agricultural Production Systems. In *Invisible Farmers: Women and the Crisis in Agriculture,* ed. Barbara Lewis, 24–102. Washington, D.C.: USAID, Office of Women in Development.

———. 1989. *Making the Case for the Gender Variable: Women and the Wealth and Well-Being of Nations.* Ed. Mari H. Clark. Washington, D.C.: USAID, Office of Women in Development.

———. 1992. *African Women in Agriculture: Farmers, Students, Extension Agents, Chiefs.* Development Studies Paper Series. Morrilton, Ark.: Winrock International Institute for Agricultural Development.

Boateng, E. Oti. 1994. Gender-Sensitive Statistics and the Planning Process. In Adepoju and Oppong 1994, 88–111.

Bohning, W. R. 1984. *Studies in International Labor Migration.* New York: St. Martin's Press.

Boserup, Ester. 1970. *Woman's Role in Economic Development.* New York: St. Martin's Press.

Boulding, Elise. 1981. Integration Into What? Reflections on Development Planning for Women. In Dauber and Cain 1981, 9–31.

Bourque, Susan C., and Kay B. Warren. 1990. Access Is Not Enough: Gender Perspectives on Technology and Education. In Tinker 1990, 83–100.

Brierley, John S. 1993. A Profile of Grenadian Women Small Farmers. In Momsen 1993b, 194–204.

Brink, Judy H. 1991. The Effect of Emigration of Husbands on the Status of Their Wives: An Egyptian Case. *International Journal of Middle East Studies* 23:201–11.

Brown, B. 1981. The Impact of Male Labor Migration on Women in Botswana. Paper presented at the Annual Meeting of the African Studies Association, October 21–24, Bloomington, Indiana.

Bruce, John W. 1989. *Community Forestry: Rapid Appraisal of Tree and Land Tenure.* Rome: UN, FAO.

Bruce, Judith, and Daisy Dwyer, eds. 1988. *A Home Divided.* Stanford, Calif.: Stanford University Press.

Brun, Thierry, Fanny Bleiburg, and Samuel Goihan. 1981. Energy Expenditure of Male Farmers in Dry and Rainy Seasons in Upper Volta. *British Journal of Nutrition* 45 (no. 67): 67–75.

Brunet-Perrault, Nicole, and Cheryl R. Doss. 1992. *Women Professionals in the Agricultural Sector: Côte d'Ivoire Case Study.* Development Studies Paper Series. Morrilton, Ark.: Winrock International Institute for Agricultural Development.

Brush, Laurie. 1986. *A Study of Female Community Development Agents in Senegal.* Tucson, Ariz.: Consortium for International Development/Women in Development Fellowship Project.

Bryceson, D. 1985. *Women and Technology in Developing Countries: Technological Change and Women's Capabilities and Bargaining Positions.* Santo Domingo, Dominican Republic: United Nations International Research and Training Institute for the Advancement of Women.

Brydon, Lynne. 1989. Gender and Rural Production. In *Women in the Third World: Gender Issues in Rural and Urban Areas,* ed. Lynne Brydon and Sylvia Chant, 69–93. Aldershot, Eng.: Edward Elgar.

Brydon, Lynne, and Sylvia Chant. 1989. *Women in the Third World: Gender Issues in Rural and Urban Areas.* Aldershot, Eng.: Edward Elgar.

Buenavista, Gladys, and Cornelia Butler Flora. 1994. Participatory Methodologies for Analyzing Household Activities, Resources, and Benefits. In Feldstein and Jiggins 1994, 36–44.

Bunch, Charlotte, and Roxanna Carrillo. 1990. Feminist Perspectives on Women in Development. In Tinker 1990, 70–82.

Burfisher, Mary E., and Nadine R. Horenstein. 1985. *Sex Roles in the Nigerian Tiv Farm Household.* West Hartford, Conn.: Kumarian Press.

Burton, Michael L., and Douglas R. White. 1984. Sexual Division of Labor in Agriculture. *American Anthropologist* 86 (3): 568–83.

Burton, Michael, Douglas White, and Malcolm Dow. 1982. *The Sexual Division of Labor in Old World Agriculture.* Women in International Development Publication Series, Working Paper No. 5. East Lansing: Michigan State University.

Buvinic, Mayra, Jennifer Sebstad, and Sandia Zeidenstein. 1979. *Credit for Rural Women: Some Facts and Lessons.* Washington, D.C.: International Center for Research on Women, for USAID, Development Support Bureau, Office of Rural Development.

Cain, Melinda. 1981. Java, Indonesia: The Introduction of Rice Processing Technology. In Dauber and Cain 1981, 127–37.

CAM (Centro Acción de las Mujeres) 1987. Fugitives from Patriarchy: The Case of Migrant Women in Guayaquil. In *Rural Women in Latin America,* ed. Isis International, 19–38. Rome: Isis International Women's Information and Communication Service.

Carloni, Alice. 1982. ESHH *Case Studies on Development Assistance in Agriculture/ Alternative Project Design.* Rome: UN, FAO.

Carloni, Alice, and Nadine Horenstein. 1986. *A Socio-Economic Assessment of the Arid and Semi-Arid Lands Project in Kenya.* Washington, D.C.: USAID, Center for Development Information and Evaluation.

Carney, Judith, and Michael Watts. 1991. Disciplining Women? Rice, Mechanization, and the Evolution of Mandinka Gender Relations in Senegambia. *Signs* 16 (4): 651–81.

Carr, Marilyn. 1978. *Appropriate Technology for African Women.* New York: UN, Economic Commission for Africa, African Training and Research Centre for Women.

———. 1984. *Blacksmith, Baker, Roofing-Sheet Maker . . . Employment for Women in Developing Countries.* London: Intermediate Technology Publications.

————. 1985. *The AT Reader: Theory and Practice in Appropriate Technology*. London: Intermediate Technology Publications.

Carr, Marilyn, ed. 1991. *Women and Food Security: The Experience of the SADCC Countries*. London: Intermediate Technology Publications.

Cashman, Kristin. 1986. The Benefits of Alley Farming for the African Farmer and Her Household. Paper presented at the International Conference on Women in Development: Gender Issues in Farming Systems Research and Extension. Gainesville: University of Florida.

CEPAL (Comisión Económica Para América Latina). 1982. *Women and Development: Guidelines for Programme and Project Planning*. Santiago, Chile: United Nations Publications.

Chakravarthy, Radha. 1992. Science, Technology and Development: The Impact on the Status of Women. In *Inventing Women: Science, Technology and Gender,* ed. Gill Kirkup and Laurie Smith Keller, 224–31. Cambridge: Polity Press.

Chambers, R., and B. P. Ghildyal. 1985. Agricultural Research for Resource-Poor Farmers: The Farmer—First and Last Model. *Agricultural Administration and Extension* 20:1–30.

Chaney, Elsa. 1980. *Women in International Migration: Issues in Development Planning.* Washington, D.C.: USAID, Office of Women in Development.

————. 1981. *Creating a Woman's Component: A Case Study on Rural Jamaica.* Washington, D.C.: USAID, Office of Women in Development.

————. 1983. *Scenarios of Hunger in the Caribbean: Migration, Decline of Smallholder Agriculture and the Feminization of Farming.* Women in Development, Working Paper No. 18. Ann Arbor: Michigan State University.

Chaney, Elsa M., and Martha Lewis. 1980. Women, Migration and the Decline of Smallholder Agriculture. Paper presented to the Board for International Food and Agricultural Development, Washington, D.C.

Chaney, Elsa M., and Marianne Schmink. 1976. Women and Modernization: Access to Tools. In *Sex and Class in Latin America,* ed. June Nash and Helen Safa, 160–82. New York: Praeger.

Chant, Sylvia. 1989. Gender and Urban Planning. In *Women in the Third World: Gender Issues in Rural and Urban Areas,* ed. Lynne Brydon and Sylvia Chant, 213–39. Aldershot, Eng.: Edward Elgar.

————. 1991. Gender, Migration and Urban Development in Costa Rica: The Case of Guanacaste. *Geoforum* 22 (3): 237–53.

————. 1992. Migration at the Margins: Gender, Poverty, and Population Movement on the Costa Rican Periphery. In *Gender and Migration in Developing Countries,* ed. Sylvia Chant, 49–72. London: Belhaven Press.

Charlton, Sue Ellen M. 1984. *Women in Third World Development*. Boulder, Colo.: Westview Press.

Chavangi, N. 1983. *Women's Role in the Livestock Sector in Africa with Special Reference to Kenya.* Rome: UN, FAO.

Chavangi, Noel A., Rutger J. Engelhard, and Valarie Jones. 1988. Culture as the Basis for Implementation of Self-Sustaining Woodfuel Development Programmes (Kenya). In *Whose Trees? Proprietary Dimensions of Forestry,* ed. Louise Fortmann and John W. Bruce, 243–53. Boulder, Colo.: Westview Press.

Chavangi, N., and A. Hanssen. 1983. *Women in Livestock Production, with Particular Reference to Dairying.* Expert Consultation on Women and Food Production. Rome: UN, FAO.

Chowdhury, Farook A., and Reazul Islam. 1988. *Intensification of Homestead Production.* Draft Report. Dhaka: World Bank.

Cloud, Kathleen. 1982. *Women and Water Management.* Tucson, Ariz.: Consortium for International Development.

———. 1984. Women's Roles in Irrigated Production Systems: Movement Toward an Integrated Approach. *The Women and Food Information Network* 2 (September): 1.

———. 1985 Women's Productivity in Agricultural Systems: Considerations for Project Design. In Overholt et al. 1985, 17–56.

———. 1986. Sex Roles in Food Production and Distribution Systems in the Sahel. In *Women Farmers in Africa: Rural Development in Mali and the Sahel,* ed. Lucy E. Creevey, 19–49. Syracuse, N.Y.: Syracuse University Press.

Colfer, Carol J. Pierce. 1994. Time Allocation Studies: A Methodological Note. In Feldstein and Jiggins 1994, 163–71.

Collins, Jane L. 1993. Gender, Contracts and Wage Work: Agricultural Restructuring in Brazil's Sao Francisco Valley. *Development and Change* 24:53–82.

Connell, J. 1984. Status or Subjugation? Women, Migration and Development in the South Pacific. *International Migration Review* 18:964–83.

Crummett, Maria de los Angeles. 1985. *Class, Household Structure, and Migration: A Case Study from Rural Mexico.* Women in International Development Publication Series, Working Paper No. 92. East Lansing: Michigan State University.

———. 1987. Rural Women and Migration in Latin America. In Deere and Leon 1987, 239–60.

Cruz, Cerenilla. 1984. *Women in Forestry: The Philippines.* Rome: UN, FAO, Tigerpapers.

Dahl, Gudrun. 1987. Women in Pastoral Production: Some Theoretical Notes on Roles and Resources. *Ethnos* 52 (1–2): 246–79.

Dankelman, Irene, and Joan Davidson. 1988. *Women and Environment in the Third World: Alliance for the Future.* London: Earthscan Publications, in association with the International Union for Conservation of Nature and Natural Resources.

Darrow, Ken, and Rick Pam. 1978. *Appropriate Technology Sourcebook.* Stanford, Calif.: Volunteers in Asia.

Date-Bah, Eugenia. 1985. Technologies for Rural Women of Ghana: Role of Sociocultural Factors. In *Technology and Rural Women: Conceptual and Empirical Factors,* ed. Iftikhar Ahmed, 211–51. London: George Allen and Unwin.

Dauber, Roslyn, and Melinda Cain, eds. 1981. *Women and Technological Change in Developing Countries.* Boulder, Colo.: Westview Press.

Davenport, Alice. 1984. *Women in Development and the Energy Sector: A Review.* Washington, D.C.: USAID.

Davenport, Alice, Tom Nickell, and Bina Pradham. 1986. *Women in Development Issues in Nepal's Resource Conservation and Utilization Project.* Washington, D.C.: USAID.

Davison, Jean, ed. 1988a. *Agriculture, Women, and Land: The African Experience.* Boulder, Colo.: Westview Press.

Davison, Jean. 1988b. Who Owns What? Land Registration and Tensions in Gender Relations of Production in Kenya. In Davison 1988a, 157–76.

Deere, Carmen Diana. 1986. Rural Women and Agricultural Reform in Peru, Chile and Cuba. In *Women and Change in Latin America,* ed. June Nash and Helen Safa, 189–207. South Hadley, Mass.: Bergin & Garvey Publishers.

———. 1990. *Household and Class Relations: Peasants and Landlords in Northern Peru.* Berkeley: University of California Press.

Deere, Carmen Diana, and Magdalena Leon, eds. 1987. *Rural Women and State Policy: Feminist Perspectives on Latin American Agricultural Development.* Boulder, Colo.: Westview Press.

Delgado, Christopher. 1979a. *The Southern Fulani Farming System in Upper Volta: A New Old Model for Integration of Crop and Livestock Production in the West African Savannah.* African Rural Economy Paper No. 20. East Lansing: University of Michigan, Department of Agricultural Economics, African Rural Economy Program.

———. 1979b. *Livestock Versus Food Grain Production in Southeast Upper Volta: A Resource Allocation Analysis.* East Lansing: University of Michigan, Center for Research on Economic Development.

Dey, Jennie. 1981. Gambian Women: Unequal Partners in Rice Development Projects? *Journal of Development Studies* 17 (3): 109–22.

———. 1984. *Women in Food Production and Food Security in Africa.* Rome: UN, FAO.

———. 1985. Women in African Rice Farming Systems. In *Women in Rice Farming Systems,* ed. International Rice Research Institute, 419–44. Aldershot, Eng.: Gower Publishing Co.

Dinnerstein, Myra. 1978. *Possible Questions and Methodological Considerations for a Survey on Women in Rural Development.* Tucson: University of Arizona, Office of Arid Lands Studies and the Title XII Committee.

Dirar, Hamid. 1992. Traditional Fermentation Technologies and Food Policy in Africa. *Appropriate Technology* 19 (3): 21–23.

Dixon, Ruth. 1980. *Assessing the Impact of Development Projects on Women.* AID Program Evaluation Discussion Paper No. 8. Washington, D.C.: USAID, Bureau for Program and Policy Coordination.

———. 1982. Women in Agriculture: Counting the Labor Force in Developing Countries. *Population and Development Review* 8 (3): 539–66.

———. 1985. *Women's Work in Third World Agriculture.* Women, Work and Development No. 9. Geneva: International Labour Office.

Dixon-Mueller, Ruth. 1985. *Women's Work in Third World Agriculture: Concepts and Indicators.* Geneva: International Labour Office.

Dixon-Mueller, Ruth, and Richard Anker. 1988. *Assessing Women's Economic Contributions to Development.* World Employment Programme, Background Papers for Training in Population, Human Resources and Development Planning, Paper No. 6. Geneva: International Labour Office.

Downing, Jeanne. 1990. *Gender and the Growth and Dynamics of Microenterprises.* GEMINI Working Paper No. 5. Washington: Growth and Equity Through Microenterprise Investments and Institutions Project (GEMINI).

Druce, Nell, and Jenny Hammond, eds. 1990. *Sweeter than Honey: Ethiopian Women and Revolution; Testimonies of Tigrayan Women.* Trenton, N.J.: Red Sea Press.

Due, Jean. 1988. Intra-Household Gender Issues in Farming Systems in Tanzania, Zambia, and Malawi. In Poats, Schmink, and Spring 1988, 331–44.

———. 1991. Policies to Overcome the Negative Effects of Structural Adjustment Programs on African Female-Headed Households. In Gladwin 1991b, 103–7.

Due, Jean M., and F. Magayane. 1990. Changes Needed in Agricultural Policy for Female-Headed Farm Families in Tropical Africa. *Agricultural Economics* 4:239–53.

Duncan, Ann, and Masooma Habib. 1988. *Women in Development: A Review of Selected Economic and Sector Reports, 1980–1987.* Washington, D.C.: World Bank, Population and Human Resources Department, Women in Development Division.

Dupire, Marguerite. 1960. The Position of Women in a Pastoral Society: The Fulani WoDaaBe, Nomads of the Niger. In *Women of Tropical Africa,* ed. Denise Paulme, 47–92. Berkeley: University of California Press.

Dwyer, Daisy Hilse. 1983. *Women and Income in the Third World: Implications for Policy.* Working Paper No. 18. New York: Population Council.

Echbal, A. 1981. *Les Femmes dans le Zone Mara-Est.* Assistance Technique au Projet de Développement de l'Elevage. Bamako, Mali: Institut au Sahel Occidental.

El-Ghonemy, M. Riad. 1993. *Land, Food and Rural Development in North Africa.* Boulder, Colo.: Westview Press.

Elmendorf, Mary L. 1980. Women, Water and Waste: Beyond Access. Arlington, Va.: Water and Sanitation for Health Project. Mimeographed.

Elmendorf, Mary L., and Raymond B. Isely. 1983. Public and Private Roles of Women in Water Supply and Sanitation Programs. *Human Organization* 42 (3): 195–204.

Ember, Carol R. 1983. The Relative Decline in Women's Contribution to Agriculture with Intensification. *American Anthropologist* 85 (2): 285–304.

Engberg, Lila E., Jean H. Sabry, and Susan A. Beckerson. 1988. A Comparison of Rural Women's Time Use and Nutritional Consequences in Two Villages in Malawi. In Poats, Schmink, and Spring 1988, 99–110.

Evans, Alison. 1992. Statistics. In Ostergaard 1992, 11–40.

Evans, Jennie. 1991. Safe Drinking Water for the Developing World. *Our Planet* 3 (1): 12–13.

Everett, Jana and Mira Savara. 1993. Organizations and Informal Sector Women Workers in Bombay. In *Gender and Political Economy: Explorations of South Asian Systems,* ed. Alice W. Clark, 273–321. Delhi: Oxford University Press.

Eviota, Elizabeth Uy. 1992. *The Political Economy of Gender: Women and the Sexual Division of Labour in the Philippines.* London: Zed Books.

FA–CIPRES. 1992. *El acceso de la mujer a la tierra en Nicaragua.* San José, Costa Rica: Fundación Arias para la Paz y el Progreso Humano, Centro para la Investigación y la Promoción del Desarrollo Rural y Social.

FAO (United Nations Food and Agriculture Organization). 1984a. *Promotion of Women's Activities in Marketing and Credit: An Analysis, Case Studies and Suggested Actions.* Rome: UN, FAO.

———. 1984b. *Women in Forestry: Thailand.* Rome: UN, FAO, Tigerpapers.

———. 1985. *Tree Growing by Rural People.* FAO Forestry Paper. Rome: UN, FAO.

———. 1990. *Women and Forestry.* Secretariat Note. Committee on Forestry, Tenth Session. Rome: UN, FAO.

———. 1991. Restoring the Balance: Women and Forest Resources. In *Women and the Environment: A Reader; Crisis and Development in the Third World,* ed. Sally Sontheimer, 67–92. New York: Monthly Review Press.

FAO/SIDA (UN, FAO, and the Swedish International Development Agency). n.d. *Restoring the Balance: Women and Forest Resources.* Uppsala, Sweden: FAO/SIDA.

Feldman, Shelley, Fazila Banu, and Florence E. McCarthy. 1986. *The Role of Rural Bangladeshi Women in Livestock Production.* Ithaca, N.Y.: Cornell University, New York State College of Agriculture and Life Sciences.

Feldstein, Hilary Sims, and Susan V. Poats, eds. 1989. *Working Together: Gender Analysis in Agriculture.* 2 vols. West Hartford, Conn.: Kumarian Press.

Feldstein, Hilary Sims, Dianne E. Rocheleau, and Louise E. Buck. 1989. Kenya: Agroforestry Extension and Research; A Case Study from Siaya District. In Feldstein and Poats 1989, 1:167–206.

Feldstein, Hilary Sims, and Janice Jiggins, eds. 1994. *Tools for the Field: Methodologies Handbook for Gender Analysis in Agriculture.* West Hartford, Conn.: Kumarian Press.

Ferrán, Fernando I., and Patricia R. Pessar. 1991. Dominican Agriculture and the Effect of International Migration. In *Small Country Development and International Labor Flows: Experiences in the Caribbean,* ed. Anthony P. Maingot, 139–65. Boulder, Colo.: Westview Press.

Feuerstein, Marie-Therese, Alexandra Shaw, and Hermoine Lovel. 1987. Editorial: The Role of Livestock in Community Development. *Community Development Journal* 22 (3): 174–88.

Finan, Timothy J., Mamadou Baro, Helen K. Henderson, and Drexel Woodson. 1991. *A Socio-Economic Study of Agricultural Villages in Guera and Batha Regions,*

Chad. Tucson: University of Arizona, Bureau of Applied Research in Anthropology.

Finlay, Barbara. 1989. *The Women of Azua: Work and Family in the Rural Dominican Republic*. New York: Praeger.

Flora, Cornelia Butler. 1985. *Appropriate Technology for Rural Women Project*. Washington, D.C.: USAID, Office of Women in Development.

Flora, Cornelia Butler, and Blas Santos. 1986. Women in Farming Systems in Latin America. In *Women and Change in Latin America,* ed. June Nash and Helen Safa, 208–28. South Hadley, Mass.: Bergin and Garvey Publishers.

Ford, Richard, Charity Kabutha, Nicholas Mageto, and Karafa Manney. 1992. *Sustaining Development Through Community Mobilization: A Case Study of Participatory Rural Appraisal in The Gambia*. Worcester, Mass.: Clark University, Program for International Development.

Fortmann, Louise. 1980. Women's Involvement in High Risk Arable Agriculture: The Botswana Case. Paper presented at the Ford Foundation Workshop on Women in Agriculture in Eastern and Southern Africa. Nairobi, Kenya.

——. 1981. The Plight of the Invisible Farmer: The Effect of National Agricultural Policy on Women. In Dauber and Cain 1981, 205–14.

——. 1982. Women's Work in a Communal Setting: The Tanzanian Policy of *Ujamaa*. In Bay 1982, 191–205.

——. 1984. Why Agroforestry Needs Women: Four Myths and a Case Study. *Unasylva* 36 (no. 146): 3–10.

——. 1985. *A Role for Women in Agroforestry Projects*. Rome: UN, FAO.

Fortmann, Louise, and John W. Bruce, eds. 1988. *Whose Trees? Proprietary Dimensions of Forestry*. Boulder, Colo.: Westview Press.

Frankenberger, Timothy R. 1985. *Adding a Food Consumption Perspective to Farming Systems Research*. Washington, D.C.: U.S. Department of Agriculture, Office of International Cooperation and Development, Nutrition Economics Group.

French, David. 1978. *Firewood in Africa*. Washington, D.C.: USAID, Africa Bureau Firewood Workshop.

FTPP (Forests, Trees and People Programme). 1989. FTP Project in Tanzania. *Forests, Trees and People Programme Newsletter* 7 (November): 24–26.

Gallin, Rita, and Anita Spring, eds. 1985. *Women Creating Wealth: Transforming Economic Development*. Washington, D.C.: Association of Women in Development Conference.

García Castro, Mary. 1986. Work Versus Life: Colombian Women in New York. In *Women and Change in Latin America,* ed. June Nash and Helen Safa, 231–59. South Hadley, Mass.: Bergin and Garvey Publishers.

Garrett, Patricia, and Patricio Espinosa. 1988. Phases of Farming Systems Research: The Relevance of Gender in Ecuadorian Sites. In Poats, Schmink, and Spring 1988, 199–212.

——. 1994. Extension Feedback and Communication: A Case from Ecuador. In Feldstein and Jiggins 1994, 207–9.

Gauch, Paula, and A. Ben David. 1983. *The Role of Women in Food Production, with Particular Reference to Small Animals at the Village Level.* Expert Consultation on Women and Food Production. Rome: UN, FAO.

Georges, Eugenia. 1990. *The Making of a Transnational Community: Migration, Development, and Cultural Change in the Dominican Republic.* New York: Columbia University Press.

Gill, Gerard J. 1991. *Seasonality and Agriculture in the Developing World: A Problem of the Poor and Powerless.* Cambridge: Cambridge University Press.

Gladwin, Christina H. 1991a. Introduction. In Gladwin 1991b, 1–22.

Gladwin, Christina H., ed. 1991b. *Structural Adjustment and African Women Farmers.* Center for African Studies. Gainesville: University of Florida Press.

———. 1993. Women and Structural Adjustment in a Global Economy. In *The Women and International Development Annual,* ed. Rita S. Gallin, Anne Ferguson, and Janice Harper, 3:87–112. Boulder, Colo.: Westview Press.

Goheen, Miriam. 1991. The Ideology and Political Economy of Gender: Women and Land in Nso, Cameroon. In Gladwin 1991b, 239–56.

Gopithath, C., and A. H. Kolaro. 1984. India: Gujarat Medium Irrigation Project. In Overholt et al. 1985, 283–308.

Goulet, Denis. 1992. Development: Creator and Destroyer of Values. *World Development* 20 (3): 467–75.

Gram Gourav Pratistan Trust. n.d. To Protect and Rehabilitate a Drought-Prone Community in Rural Maharastra, Pune, India. Mimeographed.

Guyer, Jane I. 1980. *Household Budgets and Women's Incomes.* Working Paper No. 28. Boston: Boston University, African Studies Center.

———. 1984. Naturalism in Models of African Production. *Man* 19 (3): 371–88.

———. 1991. Female Farming in Anthropology and African History. In *Gender at the Crossroads of Knowledge: Feminist Anthropology in the Postmodern Era,* ed. Micaela de Leonardo, 257–77. Berkeley: University of California Press.

Hahn, Nathalie. 1984. Losing the Land. *Development* 4:26–30.

Haile, Ferkerte. 1989. Women Fuelwood Carriers and the Supply of Household Energy in Addis Ababa. In Rathgeber 1989, 41–51.

Harry, Indra. 1993. Women in Agriculture in Trinidad: An Overview. In Momsen 1993b, 205–18.

Hartono, Soetiarti. 1984. *Women in Forestry: Indonesia.* Rome: UN, FAO, Tigerpapers.

Haugerud, Angelique. 1983. The Consequences of Land Tenure Reform Among Smallherders in the Kenya Highlands. *Rural Africana* 15–16:65–90.

Hemmings-Gapihan, Grace. 1982. International Development and the Evolution of Women's Economic Roles: A Case Study from Northern Gulma, Upper Volta. In Bay 1982, 171–89.

Henderson, Helen. 1980. The Role of Women in Livestock Production: Some Preliminary Findings. In *Upper Volta: Environmental Uncertainty and Livestock Production,* ed. R. Vengroff, 108–36. Lubbock: Texas Tech University, International Center for Arid and Semi-Arid Land Studies.

————. 1985. *Effects of More and Better Foods Dairy Component on Women.* National Academy of Science, More and Better Foods Project, Washington, D.C.; and the National Research Center, Cairo, Egypt. Tucson: University of Arizona, Bureau of Applied Research in Anthropology.

————. 1986. The Grassroots Women's Committee as a Development Strategy in an Upper Volta Village. In *Women Farmers in Africa: Development in Mali and the Sahel,* ed. Lucy E. Creevey, 133–52. Syracuse, N.Y.: Syracuse University Press.

————. 1989. *A Survey of Women's Agricultural Production and Economic Resource Bases in Eight Villages in the Brakna, Gorgol, and Guidimaka Regions.* Mauritania Agricultural Research Project II. Tucson: College of Agriculture, University of Arizona.

Henderson, Helen, Judith Warner, and Nancy Ferguson. 1982. *Women in Upper Volta.* Unpublished Preliminary Working Paper No. 2. Tucson, Ariz.: Consortium for International Development, Women in Development Project.

Henn, Jeanne Koopman. 1983. Feeding the Cities and Feeding the Peasants: What Role for Africa's Women Farmers? *World Development* 11 (no. 12): 1043–55.

Henshall, Janet D. 1981. Women and Small-Scale Farming in the Caribbean. In *Papers in Latin American Geography in Honor of Lucia C. Harrison,* ed. C. Harrison and O. Horst, 44–56. Muncie, Ind.: Conference of Latin Americanist Geographers.

Hildebrand, P., and F. Poey. 1985. *On-Farm Agronomic Trials in Farming Systems Research and Extension.* Boulder, Colo.: Lynne Reinner Press.

Hill, Polly. 1972. *Rural Hausa: A Village and a Setting.* London: Cambridge University Press.

Horn, Nancy, and Brenda Nkambule-Kanyima. 1984. *Resource Guide, Women in Agriculture: Botswana.* East Lansing: Michigan State University, Bean/Cowpea Collaborative Research Support Program.

Horowitz, Michael. 1979. *The Sociology of Pastoralism and African Livestock Projects.* AID Program Evaluation Discussion No. 6. Washington, D.C.: USAID.

Hoskins, Marilyn. 1979. *Women in Forestry for Local Community Development: A Programming Guide.* Washington, D.C.: USAID.

————. 1982. Social Forestry in West Africa: Myths and Realities. Presented at the Annual Meeting of the American Association of Science, Washington, D.C.

————. 1984. Case Study on Women, Natural Resources and Energy in International Development. In *Gender Issues in International Development Programs: A Three Part Training Program on Women in World Development,* ed. Mary Hill Rojas, 52–60. Washington, D.C.: USAID, Board for International Food and Agricultural Development.

————. n.d. *Appropriate Technology Efforts in the Field: Issues Reconsidered.* Part II: *Household Level Appropriate Technology for Women.* Washington, D.C.: U.S. Agency for Women in Development, Office of Women in Development.

Hoskins, M., and F. Weber 1985. Why Appropriate Technology Projects for Women Fail. *Ecoforum* (Environment Liaison Centre, Nairobi, Kenya) 10 (2): 6–8, 18.

Howard-Merriam, Kathleen. 1986. The Village Bank Reaches the Farm Woman: A Case from Egypt. Paper presented at the Gender Issues in Farming Systems Research and Extension Conference, University of Florida.

ICRAF (International Council for Research in Agro-Forestry). 1983. *Resources for Agro-Forestry Diagnosis and Design.* Working Paper No. 7. Nairobi: ICRAF.

ILO (International Labour Office). 1994. *The Work of Strangers: A Survey of International Labor Migration.* Geneva: International Labour Office.

INSTRAW (United Nations International Research and Training Institute for the Advancement of Women). 1989a. *Women, Water Supply and Sanitation: Making the Link Stronger.* Santo Domingo, Dominican Republic: INSTRAW.

———. 1989b. *INSTRAW News: Women and Development.* No. 13 (Winter).

———. 1991. Women, Water and Sanitation. In *Women and the Environment: A Reader; Crisis and Development in the Third World,* ed. Sally Sontheimer, 119–32. New York: Monthly Review Press.

ICRW (International Center for Research on Women) 1979. *Women in Migration: A Third World Focus.* Washington, D.C.: USAID, Office of Women in Development.

Illo, Jeanne Frances I. 1988. *Irrigation in the Philippines: Impact on Women and Their Households: The Aslong Project Case.* Bangkok, Thailand: Population Council, Regional Office for South and East Asia.

Ishak, Y., Z. El Tobshy, N. Hassan, and C. Brown. 1985. *The Role of Women in Field Crops Production and Related Information: A Research Report.* Government of Egypt, Ministry of Agriculture, Egypt Major Cereals Improvement Project. USAID, Publication No. 91. Las Cruces: New Mexico State University.

Isikdag, Fatma. 1985. Women as the Captive Labor Force: The Gezira Scheme, Sudan. In Gallin and Spring 1985, 125–28.

ISIS (Women's International Information and Communication Service). 1984. *Women in Development: A Resource Guide for Organization and Action.* Philadelphia: New Society Publishers.

Islam, Mahmuda, and Perveen Ahmad. 1984. Bangladesh: Tradition Reinforced. In *Women in the Villages, Men in the Towns,* ed. UNESCO, 21–74. New York: United Nations.

Jackson, Cecile. 1985. *The Kano River Irrigation Project.* Hartford, Conn.: Kumarian Press.

Jain, Shobita. 1991. Standing Up for Trees: Women's Role in the Chipko Movement. In *Women and the Environment, A Reader: Crisis and Development in the Third World,* ed. Sally Sontheimer, 163–78. New York: Monthly Review Press.

Jeffers, Hilde. 1983. Organizing Self-Employed Women in the Informal Sector: The Role of Innovative Credit Programs. In *Women and Work in the Third World: The Impact of Industrialization and Global Economic Interdependence,* ed. Nagat M. El-Sanabary, 299–309. Berkeley: University of California at Berkeley, Center for the Study, Education and Advancement of Women.

Jhabvala, Renana. 1994. Self-Employed Women's Association: Organising Women by Struggle and Development. In *Dignity and Daily Bread: New Forms of Economic*

Organising Among Poor Women in the Third World and the First, ed. Sheila Row-botham and Swasti Mitter, 114–38. London: Routledge.

Jiggins, Janice. 1984. *Promotion of Women's Activities in Marketing and Credit: An Analysis, Case Studies and Suggested Actions.* Rome: UN, FAO.

Johnson, Allen. 1990. Time-Allocation Research: The Costs and Benefits of Alternative Methods. In *Intra-household Resource Allocation: Issues and Methods for Development Policy and Planning,* ed. Beatrice Lorge Rogers and Nina P. Schloss-man, 140–55. Tokyo: United Nations University Press.

Jones, Christina C. 1981. Women's Legal Access to Land. In *Invisible Farmers: Women and the Crisis in Agriculture,* ed. Barbara Lewis, 197–238. Washington, D.C.: USAID, Office of Women in Development.

Jones, Christine W. 1982. *Women's Labor Allocation and Irrigated Rice Production in North Cameroon.* Jakarta, Indonesia: International Association of Agricultural Economists.

———. 1983. *The Impact of the SEMRY I Irrigated Rice Production Project on the Organization of Production and Consumption at the Intra-household Level.* USAID Contract No. PTR-0096-00-2232-00.

———. 1985. The Mobilization of Women's Labor for Cash Crop Production: A Game Theoretic Approach. In *Women in Rice Farming Systems,* ed. International Rice Research Institute, 445–54. Aldershot, Eng.: Gower Publishing Co.

Josserand, Henri P., and Edgar Ariza-Niño. 1982. The Marketing of Small Ruminants in West Africa. In *Proceedings of the Third International Conference on Goat Production and Disease.* Scottsdale, Ariz.: Dairy Goat Journal Publishing Co.

Judd, Ellen R. 1994. *Gender and Power in Rural North China.* Stanford, Calif.: Stanford University Press.

Kantara, Coulibaly Emilie. 1986. Training of Rural Women with the Stock-Farming Development Project in Western Sahel. In *Women Farmers in Africa: Rural Development in Mali and the Sahel,* ed. Lucy E. Creevey, 117–31. Syracuse, N.Y.: Syracuse University Press.

Katzin, M. H. 1959. The Jamaican Country Higgler. *Social and Economic Activities* 8 (4): 421–35.

Kennedy, Eileen, and Bruce Cogill. 1982. *Effects of Commercialization of Agriculture on Women's Decision Making and Time Allocation.* Washington, D.C.: International Food Policy Research Institute and the Association of Women in Development.

Kettel, Bonnie. 1989. Women and Milk in African Herding Systems. In Rathgeber 1989, 87–101.

Klaufert, Patricia Leyland. n.d. Women, Migration and Rural Change in Tsito. University of Birmingham, Center of West African Studies. Unpublished paper.

Kneerim, Jill. 1980. *Village Women Organize: The Mraru Bus Service.* New York: Seeds.

Kumar, Shubh. 1978. *The Role of Household Economy in Child Nutrition at Low Incomes: A Case Study in Kerala.* Occasional Paper No. 95. Ithaca, N.Y.: Cornell University, Department of Agricultural Economics.

Kumar, Shubh K., and David Hotchkiss. 1988. *Consequences of Deforestation for Women's Time Allocation, Agricultural Production, and Nutrition in Hill Areas of Nepal.* Washington, D.C.: International Food Policy Research Institute.

Ladipo, Patricia. 1991. Looking Beyond the Farm for Gender Issues in FSRE. *Journal for Farming Systems Research-Extension* 2 (2): 39–49.

Lagemann, J. 1977. *Traditional African Farming Systems in Eastern Nigeria.* Munich: Weltforum Verlag.

Lazreg, Marnia. 1990. Women, Work and Social Change in Algeria. In *Women, Employment and the Family in the International Division of Labour,* ed. Sharon Stichter and Jane L. Parpart, 183–97. Macmillan International Political Economy Series. London: Macmillan.

Leesburg, July, and Emperatriz Valencia Chavez. 1994. The *Juego de Registro.* In Feldstein and Jiggins 1994, 179–90.

Lockwood, Victoria S. 1993. *Tahitian Transformation: Gender and Capitalist Development in a Rural Society.* Boulder, Colo.: Lynne Rienner Publishers.

Lycette, Margaret. 1984. *Improving Women's Access to Credit in the Third World: Policy and Project Recommendations.* Occasional Paper No. 1. Washington, D.C.: International Center for Research on Women.

Lycette, Margaret, and Karen White. 1989. Improving Women's Access to Credit in Latin America and the Caribbean: Policy and Project Recommendations. In Berger and Buvinic 1989, 19–44.

Maathai, Wangari. 1988. *The Green Belt Movement: Sharing the Approach and the Experience.* Nairobi: Environment Liaison Centre International.

MacCormack, Carol. 1982. Control of Land, Labor, and Capital in Rural Southern Sierra Leone. In Bay 1982, 35–53.

MacKenzie, Fiona. 1985. Land and Territory: The Interface Between Two Systems of Land Tenure, Murang'a District, Kenya. *Africa* 59 (1): 91–109.

Manuh, Takyiwaa. 1989. Women, the Law and Land Tenure in Africa. In Rathgeber 1989, 26–40.

Martin, Susan Forbes. 1991. *Refugee Women.* London: Zed Books.

Massiah, Joycelin. 1993. Indicators for Planning for Women in Caribbean Development. In *Women in Developing Economies: Making Visible the Invisible,* ed. Joycelin Massiah, 11–133. Oxford: Berg Publishers.

Mathew, Brian. 1991. The Planner Manager's Guide to Third World Water Projects. In Wallace 1991a, 190–91.

Mazumdar, Vina, and Kumud Sharma. 1990. Sexual Division of Labor and the Subordination of Women: A Reappraisal from India. In Tinker 1990, 185–97.

McCall, Michael. 1987. Carrying Heavier Burdens but Carrying Less Weight: Some Implications of Villagization for Women in Tanzania. In Momsen and Townsend 1987, 192–214.

McCarthy, Florence E. 1993. Development from Within: Forms of Resistance to Development Processes Among Rural Bangladeshi Women. In *Gender and*

Political Economy: Explorations of South Asian Systems, ed. Alice W. Clark, 322–53. Delhi: Oxford University Press.

McKay, Lesley. 1993. Women's Contribution to Tourism in Negril, Jamaica. In Momsen 1993b, 278–86.

McMillan, Della. 1980. Land Tenure and Resettlement in Upper Volta. Paper presented at the Workshop on Sahelian Agriculture. West Lafayette, Ind.: Purdue University.

McSweeney, Brenda Gael. 1979a. Collection and Analysis of Data on Rural Women's Time Use. In Zeidenstein 1979, 379–83.

———. 1979b. The Negative Impact of Development on Women Reconsidered. Ph.D. diss., Fletcher School of Law and Diplomacy.

McSweeney, Brenda Gael, and Marion Freedman. 1980. Lack of Time as an Obstacle to Women's Education: The Case of Upper Volta. *Comparative Education Review* 24 (2, pt. 2): S124–S139.

Meena, Ruth. 1991. The Impact of Structural Adjustment Programs on Rural Women in Tanzania. In Gladwin 1991b, 169–90.

Meertens, Donny. 1993. Women's Roles in Colonisation: A Colombian Case Study. In *Different Places, Different Voices: Gender and Development in Africa, Asia and Latin America,* ed. Janet H. Momsen and Vivian Kinnaird, 256–77. London: Routledge.

Mencher, Joan. 1985. The Forgotten Ones: Female Landless Laborers in Southern India. In Gallin and Spring 1985, 119–23.

———. 1993. Women, Agriculture and the Sexual Division of Labour: A Three-State Comparison. In Raju and Bagchi 1993, 99–117.

Mencher, Joan, K. Saradamoni, and Janacki Panicker. 1979. Women in Rice Cultivation: Some Research Tools. In Zeidenstein 1979, 408–12.

Mezzera, Jaime. 1989. Excess Labor Supply and the Urban Informal Sector: An Analytical Framework. In Berger and Buvinic 1989, 45–64.

Mitter, Swasti. 1994. On Organising Women in Casualised Work: A Global Overview. In *Dignity and Daily Bread: New Forms of Economic Organising Among Poor Women in the Third World and the First,* ed. Sheila Rowbotham and Swasti Mitter, 14–52. London: Routledge.

Molyneaux, Maxine D. 1985. Mobilization Without Emancipation? Women's Interests, State, and Revolution in Nicaragua. *Feminist Studies* 11 (2): 227–54.

Momsen, Janet Henshall. 1991. *Women and Development in the Third World.* London: Routledge.

———. 1992. Gender Selectivity in Caribbean Migration. In *Gender and Migration in Developing Countries,* ed. Sylvia Chant, 73–90. London: Belhaven Press.

———. 1993a. Introduction. In Momsen 1993b, 1–11.

Momsen, Janet Henshall, ed. 1993b. *Women and Change in the Caribbean: A Pan-Caribbean Perspective.* Kingston, Jamaica: Ian Randle.

Momsen, Janet Henshall, and Janet G. Townsend. 1987. Towards a Geography of Gender in Developing Market Economies. In Momsen and Townsend 1987, 27–81.

Momsen, Janet Henshall, and Janet G. Townsend, eds. 1987. *Geography of Gender in the Third World.* Albany: State University of New York Press.

Monk, Janice, and C. S. Alexander. 1986. Free Port Fallout: Gender, Employment, and Migration; Margarita Island. *Annals of Tourism Research* 13 (3): 393–413.

Monk, Janice. 1993. Migration, Development and the Gender Division of Labour: Puerto Rico and Margarita Island, Venezuela. With Charles S. Alexander. In Momsen 1993b, 167–77.

Monk, Janice, and Janet Momsen. 1994. Gender and Geography in a Changing World. *Bulletin of the International Geographical Union* 44:12–19.

Moock, Peter. 1976. The Efficiency of Women as Farm Managers: Kenya. *American Journal of Agricultural Economics* 58 (5): 831–35.

Moris, Jon R. and Derrick J. Thom. 1990. *Irrigation Development in Africa: Lessons of Experience.* Studies in Water Policy and Management, No. 14. Boulder, Colo.: Westview Press.

Morna, Colleen Lowe, Ben Ephson, Souleymane Quattara, and Daphne Topouzis. 1990a. Women Farmers Emerge from the Shadows. *African Farmer* 3 (April): 23–28.

Morna, Colleen Lowe, Ben Ephson, George Kawule, Souleymane Quattara, and Shannon Horst. 1990b. Credit: A Key Agricultural Input. *African Farmer* 3 (April): 29–33.

Moser, Caroline. 1989. Gender Planning in the Third World: Meeting Practical and Strategic Gender Needs. *World Development* 17 (no. 11): 1799–1825.

———. 1993. *Gender Planning and Development: Theory, Practice and Training.* London: Routledge.

Mosse, Julia Cleves. 1993. *Half the World, Half a Chance: An Introduction to Gender and Development.* Oxford: Oxfam.

Murphey, Josette, and Leendert H. Sprey. 1980. *Evaluation socio-économique d'un projet de colonisation en Haute Volta.* AID/AFR-C-1257. Ouagadougou, Upper Volta: L'Autorité des Aménagements des Vallées des Volta.

Nash, June. 1988. Implications of Technological Change for Household and Rural Development: Some Latin American Cases. In *Lucha: The Struggles of Latin American Women,* ed. Connie Weil, 37–71. Minneapolis: Prisma Institute.

Nash, June, and Helen Safa, eds. 1986. *Women and Change in Latin America.* South Hadley, Mass.: Bergin & Garvey Publishers, Inc.

Netting, Robert McC. 1993. *Smallholders, Householders: Farm Families and the Ecology of Intensive, Sustainable Agriculture.* Stanford, Calif.: Stanford University Press.

Newman, Jeanne S. 1984. *Women in the World: Sub-Saharan Africa.* Washington, D.C.: U.S. Department of Commerce, Bureau of the Census.

Ng, Cecilia. 1991. Malay Women and Rice Production in West Malaysia. In *Women, Development and Survival in the Third World,* ed. Haleh Afshar, 188–210. London: Longman.

Niamir, Maryam. 1990. *Herders' Decision-Making in Natural Resources Management in Arid and Semi-Arid Africa.* Rome: UN, FAO.

Noble, Amanda, and Michael Nolan. 1983. *Sociological Constraints and Social Possibilities for Production of Goats in Western Kenya.* Small Ruminant Collaboration Research Support Program, Technical Report Ser. 18. Washington, D.C.: USAID.

Norem, Margaret, Sandra Russo, Marie Sambou, and Melanie Marlett. 1988. The Women's Program of the Gambian Mixed Farming Project. In Poats, Schmink, and Spring 1988, 303–13.

Noronha, Raymond, and Francis J. Lethem. 1983. *Traditional Land Tenures and Land Use Systems in the Design of Agricultural Projects.* World Bank Staff Working Paper, no. 561. Washington, D.C.: World Bank.

Obbo, Christine. 1990. East African Women, Work, and the Articulation of Dominance. In Tinker 1990, 210–22.

Oblepias-Ramos, Lilia. 1991. Does Technology Work for Women Too? In *The Role of Women in the Development of Science and Technology in the Third World,* ed. A. M. Faruqui, M.H.A. Hassan and G. Sandri, 161–66. Singapore: World Scientific.

Ogana, Winnie. 1989. Kenya: The Water that Brings New Life. In *Against All Odds: Breaking the Poverty Trap,* Harry Bhaskara, Darryl D'Monte, Nurul Huda, John Mukela, Dorothy Munyakho, Anthony Ngaiza, Winnie Ogana, Usha Rai, and Mallika Wanigasundara, contributors, 112–30. London: Panos Publications.

Ogbe, Olatokunbo A. 1989. Women and Water Resources Management in Africa. In Rathgeber 1989, 58–66.

Okali, C., and J. E. Sumberg. 1986. Sheep and Goats, Men and Women: Household Relations and Small Ruminant Production in Southwest Nigeria. In *Understanding Africa's Rural Households and Farming Systems,* ed. Joyce Lewinger Moock, 166–81. Boulder, Colo.: Westview Press.

Okonjo, Kamene. 1979. Rural Women's Credit Systems: A Nigerian Example. In Zeidenstein 1979, 326–31.

Ostergaard, Lise, ed. 1992. *Gender and Development: A Practical Guide.* London: Routledge.

Otero, Maria. 1987. *Guidebook for Integrating Women into Small and Micro Enterprise Projects.* The Gender Manual Series. Washington, D.C.: USAID, Office of Women and Development.

———. 1989. Solidarity Group Programs: A Working Methodology for Enhancing the Economic Activities of Women in the Formal Sector. In Berger and Buvinic 1989, 83–101.

Overholt, Catherine, Mary B. Anderson, Kathleen Cloud, and James E. Austin. 1985. *Gender Roles in Development Projects.* West Hartford, Conn.: Kumarian Press.

Owusu-Bempah, Kofi. 1986. The Role of Women Farmers in the Choosing of Species for Agroforestry Farming Systems in Rural Areas of Ghana. Paper presented at the International Conference on Women in Development: Gender Issues in Farming Systems Research and Extension. Gainesville: University of Florida.

Oxby, Clare. 1991. The Involvement of Agropastoralist Women in Livestock Programmes. In Wallace 1991a, 202–9.

Pala, Achola L. 1976. *African Women in Rural Development: Research Trends and Priorities.* Overseas Liaison Committee Paper No. 12. American Council on Education.

Palmer, Ingrid. 1979. *The NEMOW Case: Case Studies of the Impact of Large Scale Development Projects on Women: A Series for Planners.* New York: Population Council.

———. 1985. *The Impact of Agrarian Reform on Women.* The Population Council, Women's Roles and Gender Differences in Development Series. West Hartford, Conn.: Kumarian Press.

Pankhurst, Donna, and Susie Jacobs. 1988. Land Tenure, Gender Relations, and Agricultural Production: The Case of Zimbabwe's Peasantry. In Davison 1988a, 202–27.

Pankhurst, Helen. 1992. *Gender, Development and Identity: An Ethiopian Study.* London: Zed Books.

Paolisso, Michael, and Sally W. Yudelman. 1991. *Women, Poverty and the Environment in Latin America.* Washington, D.C.: International Center for Research on Women.

Papanek, Hanna. 1990. To Each Less than She Needs, From Each More than She Can Do: Allocation, Entitlements, and Value. In Tinker 1990, 162–81.

Paris, Thelma R. 1989a. Philippines: Women in Rice Farming Systems Crop–Livestock Project, Sta. Barbara, Pangasinan. In Feldstein and Poats 1989, 1:209–39.

———. 1989b. Philippines: Part 2–The Second Season, Experimentation and Innovation After the Introduction of the Women's Component. In Feldstein and Poats 1989, 2:204–24.

Peacock, Nadine R. 1991. Rethinking the Sexual Division of Labor: Reproduction and Women's Work Among the Efe. In *Gender at the Crossroads of Knowledge: Feminist Anthropology in the Postmodern Era,* ed. Micaela de Leonardo, 339–60. Berkeley: University of California Press.

Pearson, Anne. 1991. Animal Power: Matching Beast and Burden. *Appropriate Technology* 18 (3): 11–14.

Peluso, Nancy Lee. 1979. Collecting Data on Women's Employment in Rural Java. In Zeidenstein 1979, 374–78.

Perez-Aleman, Paola. 1992. Economic Crisis and Women in Nicaragua. In Benería and Feldman 1992, 239–58.

Peters, Pauline E. 1986. Household Management in Botswana: Cattle, Crops, and Wage Labor. In *Understanding Africa's Rural Households and Farming Systems,* ed. Joyce Lewinger Moock, 133–54. Boulder, Colo.: Westview Press.

Pezullo, Caroline. 1982. *Women and Development: Guidelines for Programme and Project Planning.* Santiago, Chile: CEPAL/United Nations.

Poats, Susan V., Marianne Schmink, and Anita Spring, eds. 1988. *Gender Issues in Farming Systems Research and Extension.* Westview Special Studies in Agriculture Science and Policy. Boulder, Colo.: Westview Press.

Potash, Betty. 1985. Female Farmers, Mothers-in-Law, and Extension Agents: Development Planning and a Rural Luo Community in Kenya. In Gallin and Spring 1985, 55–60.

Pulsipher, Lydia Mihelic. 1993. Changing Roles in the Life Cycles of Women in Traditional West Indian Houseyards. In Momsen 1993b, 50–64.

Radcliffe, Sarah A. 1992. Mountains, Maidens and Migration: Gender and Mobility in Peru. In *Gender and Migration in Developing Countries,* ed. Sylvia Chant, 30–48. London: Belhaven Press.

Rai, Usha. 1989. India: No Longer Need They Abandon Home. In *Against All Odds: Breaking the Poverty Trap,* Harry Bhaskara, Darryl D'Monte, Nurul Huda, John Mukela, Dorothy Munyakho, Anthony Ngaiza, Winnie Ogana, Usha Rai, and Mallika Wanigasundara, contributors, 88–110. London: Panos Publications.

Raikes, P. L. 1981. *Livestock Development and Policy in East Africa.* Uppsala: Scandinavian Institute of African Studies.

Raintree, J. B. 1987. *D & D User's Manual: An Introduction to Agroforestry Diagnosis and Design.* Nairobi, Kenya: International Council for Research in Agroforestry.

Raju, Saraswati, and Deipica Bagchi, eds. 1993. *Women and Work in South Asia: Regional Patterns and Perspectives.* London: Routledge.

Rao, Aruna, Mary B. Anderson, and Catherine A. Overholt. 1991. *Gender Analysis in Development Planning: A Case Book.* West Hartford, Conn.: Kumarian Press.

Rassam, Andree, and Dennis Tully. 1988. Gender Related Aspects of Agricultural Labor in Northwestern Syria. In Poats, Schmink, and Spring 1988, 287–301.

Rathgeber, Eva M., ed. 1989. *Women's Role in Natural Resource Management in Africa.* Ottawa: International Development Research Centre.

———. 1990. WID, WAD, GAD: Trends in Research and Practice. *Journal of Developing Areas* 24 (July): 489–502.

Reichman, Rebecca. 1989. Women's Participation in Two PVO Credit Programs for Microenterprise: Cases from the Dominican Republic and Peru. In Berger and Buvinic 1989, 132–60.

Reno, Barbara, ed. 1981. *Credit and Women's Economic Development.* Washington, D.C.: World Council of Credit Unions.

Reynolds, Dorene. 1982. Household Level Analysis in Economic and Political Research: A Re-evaluation with African Evidence. Paper presented at the 81st Annual Meeting of the American Anthropological Association, Washington, D.C.

Richards, Paul. 1983. Farming Systems and Agrarian Change in West Africa. *Progress in Human Geography* 7 (1): 1–39.

Roark, Paula. 1980. *Social Soundness: Upper Volta Village Water Supply Design Project.* Washington, D.C.: USAID, Office of Women in Development.

Robson, Emma. 1991. From Provider to Promoter: Gambia's Rocky Transition. *Source* 3 (2): 10–13.

Rocheleau, Dianne E. 1988. Women, Trees, and Tenure: Implications for Agroforestry. In *Whose Trees? Proprietary Dimensions of Forestry,* ed. Louise Fortmann and John W. Bruce, 254–72. Boulder, Colo.: Westview Press.

Rocheleau, Dianne, Kamoji Wachira, Luis Malaret, and Bernard Muchiri Wanjohi. 1989. Local Knowledge for Agroforestry and Native Plants. In *Farmer First:*

Farmer Innovation and Agricultural Research, ed. Robert Chambers, Arnold Pacey, and Lori Ann Thrupp, 14–24. London: Intermediate Technology Publications.

Rodale, Robert. 1991. *Save Three Lives: A Plan for Famine Prevention.* San Francisco: Sierra Club Books.

Rodda, Annabel. 1991. *Women and the Environment.* London: Zed Books.

Rogers, Beatrice Lorge. 1990. The Internal Dynamics of Households: A Critical Factor in Development Policy. In *Intra-household Resource Allocation: Issues and Methods for Development Policy and Planning,* ed. Beatrice Lorge Rogers and Nina P. Schlossman, 1–19. Tokyo: United Nations University Press.

Russo, Sandra, Jennifer Bremer-Fox, Susan Poats, and Laurene Graig. 1989. *Gender Issues in Agriculture and Natural Resource Management.* In cooperation with Anita Spring, edited by Bruce Horwith. Gender Manual Series. Washington, D.C.: USAID, Office of Women in Development.

Rutherford, Andy. 1987. Strengthening Livestock Rearing Practices of Marginalized Indian Women. *Community Development Journal* 22 (3): 246–50.

Safa, Helen I., and Peggy Antrobus. 1992. Women and the Economic Crisis in the Caribbean. In Benería and Feldman 1992, 49–82.

Safilios-Rothschild, Constantina. 1983. *Women in Sheep and Goat Production and Marketing.* Expert Consultation on Women and Food Production. Rome: UN, FAO.

———. 1985. The Persistence of Women's Invisibility in Agriculture: Theoretical and Policy Lessons from Lesotho and Sierra Leone. *Economic Development and Cultural Change* 33 (2): 299–318.

———. 1994. Agricultural Policies and Women Producers. In Adepoju and Oppong 1994, 54–63.

Saito, Katrine A., and Daphne Spurling. 1992. *Developing Agricultural Extension for Women Farmers.* World Bank Discussion Paper 156. Washington, D.C.: World Bank.

Saito, Katrine A., and C. Jean Weidemann. 1990. *Agricultural Extension for Women Farmers in Africa.* Policy, Research, and External Affairs Working Papers. Washington, D.C.: World Bank.

Sandhu, Ruby, and Joanne Sandler. 1986. *The Tech and Tools Book: A Guide to Technologies Women Are Using Worldwide.* London: International Women's Tribune Center, I. T. Publications.

Saradamoni, K. 1991. *Filling the Rice Bowl: Women in Paddy Cultivation.* Hyderabad, India: Sangam Books.

Saul, Mahir. 1981. Beer, Sorghum and Women: Production for the Market in Rural Upper Volta. *Africa* 5 (3): 746–64.

Schloss, Marc. 1988. *The Hatchet's Blood: Separation, Power, and Gender in Ehing Social Life.* Tucson: University of Arizona Press.

Schoepf, Brooke Grundfest, and Claude Schoepf. 1988. Land, Gender, and Food Security in Eastern Kivu, Zaire. In Davison 1988a, 106–30.

Scrimshaw, Susan C. M. 1990. Combining Quantitative and Qualitative Methods in the Study of Intra-household Resource Allocation. In *Intra-household Resource*

Allocation: Issues and Methods for Development Policy and Planning, ed. Beatrice Lorge Rogers and Nina P. Scholossman, 86–98. Tokyo: United Nations University Press.

Sen, Amartya K. 1990. Gender and Cooperative Conflicts. In Tinker 1990, 123–49.

Sen, Gita. 1982. Women Workers and the Green Revolution. In *Women and Development: The Sexual Division of Labor in Rural Societies,* ed. Lourdes Benería, 29–64. New York: Praeger.

Senauer, Benjamin. 1990. The Impact of the Value of Women's Time on Food and Nutrition. In Tinker 1990, 150–61.

Sharma, Miriam. 1984. *Caste, Class and Gender: Women's Role in Agricultural Development in North India.* Working Paper No. 57. East Lansing: Michigan State University.

Shifferaw, Maigenet. 1985. The Training Components of Women's Projects in Rural Africa: Do They Promote or Retard Women's Participation in the Development of Their Countries? In Gallin and Spring 1985, 51–53.

Shiva, Vandana. 1989. *Staying Alive: Women, Ecology and Development.* London: Zed Books.

Shobha, V. 1987. *Rural Women and Development: A Study of Female Agricultural Labourers in Telangana.* Delhi: Mittal Publications.

Shrestha, P., L. Zivetz, B. Sharma, and S. Anderson. 1984. *Planning Extension for Farm Women.* Kathmandu, Nepal: USAID, Integrated Cereals Project.

Silliman, Jael, and Roberto Lenton. 1985. Irrigation and the Land-Poor. Paper presented to the International Conference on Food and Water. Texas A & M University, College Station, May 27–30.

Singamma Sreenivasan Foundation. 1993. Integrating Women in Development Planning: The Role of Traditional Wisdom. In *Women in Developing Economies: Making Visible the Invisible,* ed. Joycelin Massiah, 280–300. Oxford: Berg Publishers.

Singhanetra-Renard, Anchalee. 1987. Non-farm Employment and Female Labour Mobility in Northern Thailand. In Momsen and Townsend 1987, 258–73.

Smale, Melinda. 1980. *Women in Mauritania: The Effects of Drought and Migration on Their Economic Status and Implications for Development Programs.* Washington, D.C.: USAID, Office of Women in Development.

Spears, J. S. 1978. Wood as an Energy Source: The Situation in the Developing World. Paper presented at the 103rd Annual Meeting of the American Forestry Association, Washington D.C.

Spindel, Cheywa R. 1987. The Social Invisibility of Women's Work in Brazilian Agriculture. In Deere and Leon 1987, 51–66.

Spiro, H. M. 1980a. *The Domestic Economy and Rural Time Budgets.* Discussion Paper 6/80. Ibadan, Nigeria: International Institute of Tropical Agriculture, Agricultural Economics Section.

―――. 1980b. *The Role of Women Farming in Oyo State, Nigeria: A Case Study in Two Rural Communities.* Discussion Paper 6/80. Ibadan: International Institute of Tropical Agriculture, Agricultural Economics Section.

Spiro, Heather. 1985. *The Ilora Farm Settlement in Nigeria.* West Hartford, Conn.: Kumarian Press.

Spring, Anita. 1986. Men and Women Smallholder Participants in a Small-Feeder Livestock Program in Malawi. *Human Organization* 45 (2): 154–62.

———. 1987. *Using Male Research and Extension Resources to Target Women Farmers.* Working Paper on Women in International Development, no. 144. East Lansing: Michigan State University.

———. 1988. Using Male Research and Extension Personnel to Target Women Farmers. In Poats, Schmink, and Spring 1988, 407–26.

Spring, Anita, Craig Smith, and Freida Kayuni. 1983. *Women Farmers in Malawi: Their Contribution to Agriculture and Participation in Development Projects.* Washington, D.C.: USAID, Office of Women in Development.

Stamp, Patricia. 1990. *Technology, Gender, and Power in Africa.* Ottawa: International Development Research Centre.

Stanbury, Pamela C. 1984. *Women's Roles in Irrigated Agriculture: 1984 Diagnostic Analysis Workshop.* Dahod Tank Irrigation Project. Madhya Pradesh, India.

Staudt, Kathleen. 1978. Agricultural Productivity Gaps: A Case Study of Male Preference in Government Policy Implementation. *Development and Change* 9:439–57.

———. 1982. Women Farmers and Inequalities in Agricultural Services. In Bay 1982, 207–24.

———. 1983. Development Interventions and Differential Technology Impact Between Men and Women. In *Vrouwen in De Derde Wereld: Energie en Aangepaste Technologie,* ed. Ilsa de Beij, 59–80. Leiden: Rijks Universiteit, Leiden.

———. 1985. *Agricultural Policy Implementation: A Case Study from Western Kenya.* West Hartford, Conn.: Kumarian Press.

Stavrakis, O., and M. I. Marshall. 1978. Women, Agriculture and Development in the Mayan Lowlands: Profit or Progress? In *Proceedings and Papers of the International Conference on Women and Food,* 3:A25–A42. Tucson, Ariz.: Consortium for International Development.

Stead, Mary. 1991. Women, War and Underdevelopment in Nicaragua. In *Women, Development and Survival in the Third World,* ed. Haleh Afshar, 53–87. London: Longman.

Stein, J. 1977. *Water: Life or Death.* Washington, D.C.: International Institute for Environment and Development.

Stenning, Derrick. 1959. *Savannah Nomads.* London: Oxford University Press.

Stevens, Yvette. 1985. Improved Technologies for Rural Women: Problems and Prospects for Rural Sierra Leone. In *Technology and Rural Women: Conceptual and Empirical Issues,* ed. Iftikhar Ahmed, 284–326. London: George Allen and Unwin.

Stichter, Sharon. 1990. Women, Employment and the Family: Current Debates. In *Women, Employment and the Family in the International Division of Labour,* ed. Sharon Stichter and Jane L. Parpart, 11–71. Macmillan International Political Economy Series. London: Macmillan.

Stoler, Ann. 1977. Class Structure and Female Autonomy in Rural Java. *Signs* 3 (1): 74–89.

Stone, M. Priscilla. 1988. Women Doing Well: A Restudy of the Nigerian Kofyar. *Research in Economic Anthropology* 10:287–306.

Suphanchaimat, Nongluk. 1994. Household Record Keeping as a Means of Understanding Farmers' Decision Making. In Feldstein and Jiggins 1994, 155–62.

Swift, Jeremy. 1991. Traditional Pastoral Milk Products in Mongolia. *Appropriate Technology* 18 (1): 14–16.

Taft, Julia Vadala. 1987. *Issues and Options for Refugee Women in Developing Countries.* Washington, D.C.: Refugee Policy Group.

Talle, Aud. 1987. Women as Heads of Houses: The Organization of Production and the Role of Women Among Pastoral Maasai in Kenya. *Ethnos* 52 (nos. 1–2): 50–80.

———. 1988. *Women at a Loss: Changes in Maasai Pastoralism and Their Effects on Gender Relations.* Stockholm: University of Stockholm.

Tavakolian, Bahram. 1987. Sheikhanzai Women: Sisters, Mothers and Wives. *Ethnos* 52 (nos. 1–2): 180–99.

Thiam, Adam. 1991. Simple Herders: Goodbye to the Good Years? *Appropriate Technology* 18 (1): 6–7.

Thompson, James T. 1980. Peasant Perceptions of Problems and Possibilities for Local-Level Management of Trees in Niger and Upper Volta. Paper presented at the Twenty-third Annual Meeting of the African Studies Association, Philadelphia, October 15–18.

Tinker, Irene. 1981. New Technologies for Food Related Activities: An Equity Strategy. In Dauber and Cain 1981, 51–88.

Tinker, Irene, ed. 1990. *Persistent Inequalities: Women and World Development.* New York: Oxford University Press.

Todaro, Michael P. 1985. *Economic Development in the Third World.* New York: Longman.

Trenchard, Esther. 1987. Rural Women's Work in Sub-Saharan Africa and the Implications for Nutrition. In Momsen and Townsend 1987, 153–72.

Tripp, Aili Mari. 1992. The Impact of Crisis and Economic Reform on Women in Urban Tanzania. In Benería and Feldman 1992, 159–80.

Turner, Jim, and Maria Suizo. 1986. Encouraging Female Participation in Irrigation Projects. Washington, D.C.: USAID, Center for Development Information and Evaluation. Mimeographed.

UN. 1991. *The World's Women, 1970–1990: Trends and Statistics.* New York: United Nations, Department of International Economic and Social Affairs, Children's Fund, Population Fund, and Development Fund for Women.

UNDP (United Nations Development Program). 1980. *Rural Women's Participation in Development.* Evaluation Study No. 3. New York: UNDP.

———. n.d. *Decade Dossier: International Drinking Water Supply and Sanitation Decade, 1981–1990.* New York: UNDP.

UNHCR (United Nations High Commissioner for Refugees). 1989. *Refugee Women: A Selected and Annotated Bibliography.* Geneva: UNHCR, Centre for Documentation on Refugees.

UN Water Conference. 1977. Water, Women and Development. Paper presented at United Nations Water Conference, Mar del Plata, Argentina, March 14–25, 1977. United Nations, Department of Social and Economic Affairs, Centre for Social Development and Humanitarian Affairs.

Unnevehr, Laurian J. 1985. Asian Women as Users and Beneficiaries of IARC Technology. In *CGIAR Inter-Center Seminar on Women and Agricultural Technology: Relevance for Research,* vol. 2. Experiences in International and National Research. New York: Rockefeller Foundation.

Uphoff, N. 1981. The Institutional Organizer (IO) Programme in the Field After Three Months: A Report on Trip to Ampare/Gal Oya, June 17–20, 1981. Cornell University, Rural Development Committee. Mimeographed.

————. 1982a. A Case Study of Learning Process Applied to Farmer Organization and Participation in Water Management: The Institutional Organizer Program in Gal Oya, Sri Lanka. Cornell Rural Development Committee. Mimeographed.

————. 1982b. The Institutional Organizer (IO) Programme in the Field After Ten Months: A Report on Trip to Ampare/Gal Oya, Sri Lanka, Jan. 14–17, 1982. Rural Development Committee, Cornell University. Mimeographed.

Vaidyanathan, A. 1983. *Estimating Employment Potential in Animal Husbandry.* Rome: UN, FAO.

Walker, S. Tjip. 1990. *Innovative Agricultural Extension for Women: A Case Study in Cameroon.* Policy, Research, and External Affairs Working Papers. Washington, D.C.: World Bank.

Wallace, Tina, ed. 1991a. *Changing Perceptions: Writings on Gender and Development.* With Candida March. Oxford: Oxfam.

Wallace, Tina. 1991b. "Taking the Lion by the Whiskers": Building on the Strengths of Refugee Women. In Wallace 1991a, 60–67.

Watson, Cathy. 1991. Turkana Women: Their Contribution in a Pastoralist Society. In Wallace 1991a, 193–201.

Watson-Franke, Maria Barbara. 1987. Women and Property in Guajiro Society. *Ethnos* 52 (nos. 1–2): 229–45.

Weidemann, C. Jean. 1991. *Egyptian Women and Microenterprise: The Invisible Entrepreneurs.* In collaboration with Zohra Merabet. Washington, D.C.: USAID, Office of Women in Development.

Weinpahl, Jan. 1984. Women's Roles in Livestock Production Among the Turkana of Kenya. *Research in Economic Anthropology* 6:193–215.

White, Karen, Maria Otero, Margaret Lycette, and Mayra Buvinic. 1986. *Integrating Women into Development Programs: A Guide for Implementation for Latin America and the Caribbean.* USAID, prepared for the Bureau for Latin America and the Caribbean.

White, Sarah C. 1992. *Arguing with the Crocodile: Gender and Class in Bangladesh.* London: Zed Books.

White, Sylvia. 1983. African Women as Small-Scale Entrepreneurs: Their Impact on Employment Creation. Paper presented at the Western Association of Africanists Annual Meeting, April 15–16, Laramie, Wyoming.

Whitehead, Ann. 1991. Food Crisis and Gender Conflict in the African Countryside. In *The Food Question: Profits Versus People?* ed. Henry Bernstein, B. Crow, and M. Mackintosh, 54–68. London: Earthscan Publications.

———. 1994. Wives and Mothers: Female Farmers in Africa. In Adepoju and Oppong 1994, 35–53.

Wickramasinghe, Anoja. 1993. Women's Roles in Rural Sri Lanka. In *Different Places, Different Voices: Gender and Development in Africa, Asia and Latin America,* ed. Janet Henshall Momsen and Vivian Kinnaird, 159–75. International Studies of Women and Place Series. London: Routledge.

Wienpahl, Jan. 1984. Women's Roles in Livestock Production Among the Turkana of Kenya. *Research in Economic Anthropology* 6:193–215.

Wiff, M. 1984. Honduras: Women Make a Start in Agroforestry. *Unasylva* 36 (no. 146): 21–26.

Wiggins, Steve. 1991. Pastoralism in Crisis. *Appropriate Technology* 18 (1): 1–4.

Wigna, Winati, Krisnawati Suryanata, and Benjamin White. 1980. *Comparison of the Results of Time-Allocation Research, Using Two Different Recall Periods.* Working Paper No. 7. Bogor, Indonesia: Agro-Economic Survey.

Wilkinson, Clive. 1987. Women, Migration and Work in Lesotho. In Momsen and Townsend 1987, 225–39.

Wollenberg, Eva. 1988. An Evaluation of Methodologies Used in Time Allocation Research. In Poats, Schmink, and Spring 1988, 127–47.

———. 1994. Selecting Methods of Time Allocation Research. In Feldstein and Jiggins 1994, 172–78.

World Bank. 1990. *Bangladesh: Strategies for Enhancing the Role of Women in Economic Development.* Washington, D.C.: World Bank.

———. 1991. *Gender and Poverty in India.* Washington, D.C.: World Bank.

Young, Kate. 1982. The Creation of a Relative Surplus Population: A Case Study from Mexico. In *Women and Development: The Sexual Division of Labor in Rural Societies,* ed. Lourdes Benería, 149–77. New York: Praeger Publications.

———. 1992. Household Resource Management. In Ostergaard 1992, 135–64.

———. 1993. *Planning Development with Women: Making a World of Difference.* London: MacMillan.

Yousef, Nadia H., and Carol B. Helter. 1983. Establishing the Economic Condition of Women-Headed Households in the Third World: A New Approach. In *Women and Poverty in the Third World,* ed. Mayra Buvinic, Margaret Lycette, and William P. McGreevey, 216–42. Baltimore: Johns Hopkins University Press.

Zeidenstein, Sondra, ed. 1979. *Learning About Rural Women.* New York: Population Council. Special Issue of *Studies in Family Planning* 10 (nos. 11–12).

Zeitlin, Marian Frank. 1990. Use of Emic Units for Time-Use Recall. In *Intra-household Resource Allocation: Issues and Methods for Development Policy and Planning,* ed. Beatrice Lorge Rogers and Nina P. Schlossman, 156–63. Tokyo: United Nations University Press.

Zimmerman, Sonja D. 1982. *The Cheese Makers of Kafr Al Bahr: The Role of Egyptian Women in Animal Husbandry and Dairy Production.* Cairo: Research Centre for Women in Development Series.

INDEX